For Ages 3 to 10, Includes
Reproducible Pages

52 **[** to Teach Children

GODtalk

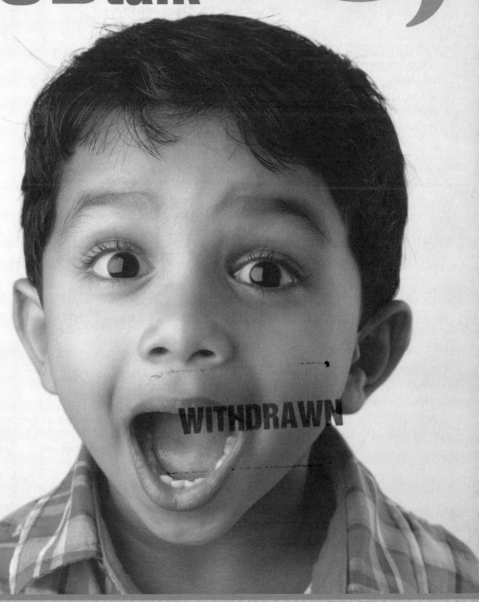

Rita B. Hays

God Talk: 52 Fun Activities to Teach Children

Writer: Rita B. Hays
Editor: Daphna Flegal
Production Editor: Karen Scholle
Designer: Keitha Vincent

Art Credits—Cover photo: Shutterstock®; p. 8: Paula Martyr/Linden Artists LTD;
pp. 14, 29, 31, 33, 48, 63, 71, 93, 97: Robert S. Jones; pp 16, 36, 39, 68, 75, 88: Megan
Jeffery; p. 24: Randy Wollenmann; p. 107: Keitha Vincent

PACP00936206-01

ISBN 978-1-426-73615-5

11 12 13 14 15 16 17 18 19 20—10 9 8 7 6 5 4 3 2 1

Printed in the U.S.A.

Table of Contents

Introduction

GODtalk: 52 Fun Ways to Teach Children About God offers teachers, parents, and leaders of children a lesson and activity for every week of the year, each centered around Scripture. The lessons are designed to teach children about God and help children apply biblical principles to their lives today. In *GODtalk*, children are invited to use their senses and engage in learning.

Each *GODtalk* lesson contains the following:
- Bible verse
- Talk Point
- God Talk conversation
- Putting God Talk Into Action (craft and activity idea)
- Prayer.

Items needed for each God Talk are listed along with any reproducibles needed for the lessons.

God Talk conversations are taken from both the Old and New Testament and include lessons for the seasons of Advent and Lent in addition to Epiphany Sunday and Pentecost Sunday.

Settings
God Talk may be used in a variety of settings within the church. Worship leaders who have the responsibility of sharing the children's sermon could, with little preparation, use the God Talk conversations in the worship setting. Children's church leaders can follow up by reinforcing the God Talk and having the children put the God Talk into action through a simple craft project and or activity, thus providing a consistency with what the children have heard in worship.

God Talk could also be used for Wednesday night children's programming, special children's events, children's devotional times, and as a supplement to Sunday school lessons.

God Talk in Families
Parents and grandparents will find *GODtalk* a helpful resource in the home to engage their children in conversations about God. Lessons can easily be adapted for use in the family setting. The craft projects will be especially fun for children, but enjoyable for all family members.

I Am a Special Creation

Bible Verse
And I praise you because of the wonderful way you created me.
(Psalm 139:14, CEV)

Talk Point
God made you and you are special.

Items Needed
small hand mirrors, glue, small flowers, shells, or stickers

God Talk
Have each child hold the mirror in front of his or her face.

God made us! We are special to God! What color are your eyes? *(Give children time to respond.)* God made your eyes and they are beautiful. What color is your hair? *(Give children time to respond.)* God made your hair and it is beautiful. Look at your face. God made your face and you are beautiful.

Put down your mirrors. Look at your hands. Let's say together: **Thank you, God, for my hands.** What are some things you do with your hands? *(play baseball, write, eat, wave)* Look at your feet? Let's say together: **Thank you, God, for my feet.** What are some things you do with your feet? *(kick a ball, walk, run, skip, jump)* God made your entire body, the inside and the outside.

Hold your mirror in front of your face. Look in the mirror. Repeat after me: **God made me. I am special! God made me beautiful!**

Putting God Talk Into Action
Purchase plain mirrors that the children can decorate. Provide small dried flowers, shells, or stickers to decorate the sides of the mirrors. Write each child's name on the back of his or her mirror.

Prayer
God, thank you for making me beautiful. Thank you for my face, body, hands, and feet. Thank you for all of me! I am a special creation! Amen.

God Shapes My Life

Bible Verse

I went there and saw the potter making clay pots on his pottery wheel. And whenever the clay would not take the shape he wanted, he would change his mind and form it into some other shape.

(Jeremiah 18:3-4, CEV)

Talk Point

God has a plan for your life. God works to shape your life in good ways.

Items Needed

play dough, craft sticks, small clay flowerpots, crayons, flower and leaf patterns (page 8)

God Talk

Encourage the children to make a small pot out of their play dough.

God asked the prophet Jeremiah to go down to the potter's shop. A prophet is a special helper of God's who speaks for God. A prophet tells people what God wants the people to do in order to serve God better. A potter is a person who works with clay and makes beautiful pots and dishes. When Jeremiah arrives at the potter's shop, he finds the potter busy making a pot. The potter is not pleased with the pot he is making. He does not like the shape, so he remakes it into another shape.

Take your play dough and smash it! Start over again. Make the pot different from the first pot you made.

Play some quiet music as the children work.

Watching the potter helped Jeremiah think about God. God shapes our lives. God shapes us into boys and girls that are pleasing to God. You are growing every day. You are changing. You are learning. God is shaping you and making you into a beautiful boy and girl. God wants to be pleased with the way you turn out. You must work with God to help God shape your life. You do this when you read your Bible, pray to God, and do the things that make God happy.

Putting God Talk Into Action

Provide the children with small clay flower pots. Put some play dough in the bottom of each pot.

Photocopy and cut out flowers and leaves *(below)* for each child. Give the children the cutouts to decorate with crayons.

Give each child a craft stick. Show the children how to glue flowers and leaves on both sides of their craft sticks. Have the children push their craft sticks into the play dough in the flowerpot.

Prayer

God, thank you for shaping my life. Thank you for the ways I am changing each day and getting bigger and stronger. Help me to grow into a boy or girl that pleases you. Amen.

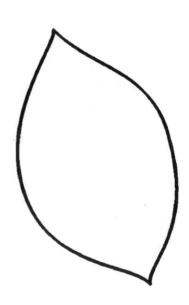

God Always Watches Over Me

Bible Verse
The LORD is your protector, and he won't go to sleep.
(Psalm 121:3, CEV)

Talk Point
To help children understand that God watches over them at all times.

Items Needed
pillows, pillowcases

God Talk
Have each child take a pillow and rest his or her head on the pillow.

We need sleep each night so our bodies can rest and wake up refreshed and ready for a new day. The Bible tells us that God never sleeps. God does not need to sleep. Rather than sleep, God spends time watching over all of us. We do not need to worry because our God cares for us. Each boy and girl is important to God. When you go to sleep at night, you do not have to be afraid. God watches over you. When you get up in the morning, you do not have to be scared. God watches over you. God protects you both day and night!

Putting God Talk Into Action
Give each child a pillowcase to decorate. Write on one side of the pillowcase, "God watches over (name of child)."

Prayer
God, I thank you for watching over me. I do not have to be afraid because I know you care for me day and night. Amen.

God Loves Me and I Love Others

Bible Verse
Dear friends, since God loved us this much, we must love each other.
(1 John 4:11, CEV)

Talk Point
God loves you and you must love others.

Items Needed
heart, red construction paper, scissors, pencils, crayons or markers

God Talk
Hold up a picture of a heart.

What am I holding in my hand? *(heart)* When you see a heart, what do you think of? *(Valentine's Day, love)* There are many people that love you. Who are some of these people? *Hand the heart to one child and ask the name of the child.* (Child's name), who loves you? *Let the child respond and have that child pass the heart to another child. Continue until all of the children are given an opportunity to say who loves them. (mother, father, brothers, sisters, teachers, pastors, grandparents, aunts, uncles, friends)*

There is someone who loves us more than anyone. That person is God. God loves us so very, very much. God's love is wonderful. God teaches us in the Bible that we are to love others. We love others because God loves us.

Putting God Talk Into Action
Give each child a piece of red construction paper. Show the children how to fold their paper in half and cut out hearts. Let the children write notes to persons they love on their hearts.

Prayer
God, thank you for loving us so much. Help us to love others. Amen.

Like Salt

Bible Verse
You are like salt for everyone on earth.

(Matthew 5:13, CEV)

Talk Point
You can show others God's love by kind and loving actions.

Items Needed
saltshaker/salt, napkins, pencils, slips of paper, empty saltshakers (one per child)

God Talk

Give each child a napkin. Pass the saltshaker around to each child. Let the child shake some salt onto his or her napkin.

Salt is used to flavor food. Jesus teaches us that we are like salt for other people. Jesus meant that just as salt makes food taste better, we can help others have better lives by showing them God's love. We can flavor the lives of others with kind and loving actions. What are some things you can do to show God's love to others? (*be kind, share, be patient, listen to my teachers, love others, help people*) Each time a child names something, have the children take a pinch of salt in their fingers and let it go as everyone says to the child who shared, "You are like salt."

Putting God Talk Into Action
Give the children small slips of paper. Instruct each child to write one of the ideas for ways to show God's love to others on each slip of paper. Have the children place their slips of paper in the saltshakers and take them home.

Prayer
Like salt makes food better, I want to make my world a better place. Jesus, you ask me to do this and I know you will help me. Amen.

God Talk Reminder
Preschool children may not understand the concept of salt as it applies to our lives as Christians. They can understand how to show love.

God Knows My Name!

Bible Verse
I have called you by name; now you belong to me.
(Isaiah 43:1, CEV)

Talk Point
God knows your name and you belong to a loving God.

Items Needed
foam door hangers, foam religious stickers (peel-off), baby name book, markers

God Talk

Have children look up the meaning of their names in a baby book or on computer. You might look up some names and have the meanings ready for the children.

Our names are important. Do you know how you got your name? Were you named after someone in your family? *(Give time for the children to discuss.)* Each of our names has a meaning. What does your name mean? *(Try to say something affirming after each child shares what his or her name means.)*

The Bible tells us that God knows our names. Isn't that wonderful? God does not just know that we are a boy or girl, but God knows our names and what they mean. God loves us so much that God takes the time to learn our names. God wants to know everything about us. Our names are special. By knowing our names, God tells us that we belong to a loving God.

Putting God Talk Into Action
Purchase foam door hangers at a craft or hobby store. Have the children write their names on the door hangers with markers. Decorate the door hangers with the religious stickers.

Prayer
God, I am so glad you know my name! I am special to you. I belong to you. You show your love for me by learning my name. Thank you. Amen.

God Loves the World

Bible Verse
God loved the people of the world so much that he gave his only Son, so that everyone who has faith in him will have eternal life and never really die.
(John 3:16, CEV)

Talk Point
God loves the entire world and God proved this love by sending Jesus.

Items Needed
globe, glue, construction paper, magazines, picture of the world (page 14), scissors

God Talk

Spin the globe and have each child, one at a time, place his or her finger on the globe to stop it spinning. Have each child tell you what country his or her finger landed on. Have the children say, "God loves the people of (country)."

God loves all the people and nations of the world. God does not love one group of people and one country more than the others. God loves all of us.

The people of our world speak many different languages. They have customs and celebrations that are unique to their countries. Some people dress differently from you and me. This does not mean that God loves these people any less because they are different from us. God loves the people of the world who have light skin and dark skin. Skin color does not matter to God.

God loves all of the people of the world because they are God's children. We must learn to love others even when they live in a different country from us. God sent Jesus into the world to show all of the nations of the world that they are loved.

Putting God Talk into Action
Give each child a piece of construction paper. Photocopy and cut out the picture of the world (page 14) for each child. Let him or her glue the picture of the world on the construction paper. Have him or her write over the picture of the world, "God loves the world."

Encourage the children to look through magazines and cut out pictures of different people. Have the children glue these pictures around the pictures of the world to indicate some of the persons that God loves.

Prayer

God, thank you for loving all of the people of the world. Thank you for loving us. Amen.

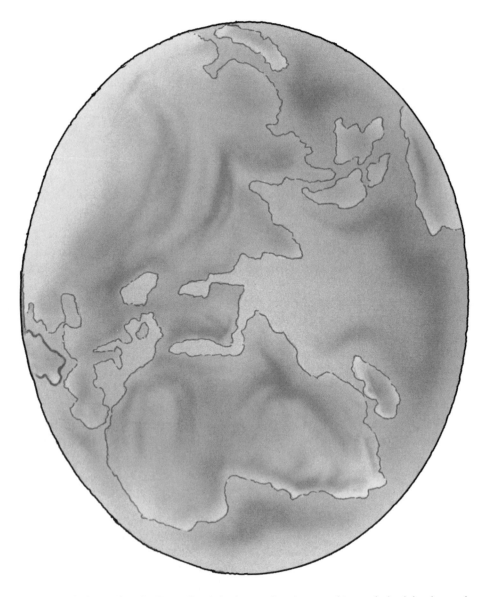

A Time for Everything

Bible Verse

Everything on earth has its own time and its own season.
(Ecclesiastes 3:1, CEV)

Talk Point

God is with us all the time.

Items Needed

clock, small paper plates, clock hands (page 16), brads, markers or crayons, scissors

God Talk

Show the children the clock.

A clock tells us the time. According to my clock the time right now is
_____. A clock helps us know when it is the exact time to do certain
things or go certain places. What else might we use to help us tell time?
(watch, computer, cell phone) All of these tell us the time so that we will not
be late to the places we need to go or we will not be tardy in doing our
chores. Tell me some of the things you do or the places you go where you
must arrive at the correct time and not be late. *(catching the bus for school,
arriving at school, arriving at Sunday school or church, arriving at practice for
sporting event or other activity, going to bed)*

The Bible tells us that there is a time for everything. There is a time to be
born. There is a time to die. There is a time for crying, but also a time to
be happy. There is a time for listening, but also a time for speaking. Now
is the time when you are a child, but one day you will be a teenager, and
then an adult. As time passes, you will change, grow, and learn many
new things. You will have many different experiences in life. Sometimes
you will be happy, but other things you will be sad. Some of your times
will be good times and others will be hard times. God stays with us in all
of the times of life. God helps us in every time of our life. Whatever
happens to you or whatever the time, God is always with you.

Putting God Talk Into Action

Give each child a small paper plate. Photocopy and cut out the clock hands and give each child a set. Have the child write the numbers on the plate like the numbers on a clock. Help the child fasten the hands on the clock using a brad.

When you call out a time, the children will move the hands of the clock to that time. Say: "What time is it?" Have the children respond, "God's time!" Do this several times.

God Talk Reminder

Let preschoolers make their clocks without numbers. Tell them to move the hands on the clock when you say "go" and to stop moving the hands on their clock when you say "stop." When they stop moving the clock hand, say "What time is it?" Preschool children can respond "God's time!" Give them stickers to place on their clocks. Repeat until the children have several stickers on their clocks.

Prayer

Thank you, God, that you are with us at all times. Amen.

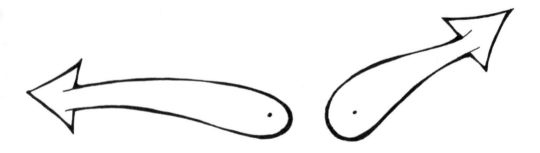

16

God Made the World

Bible Verse
In the beginning God created the heavens and the earth.
(Genesis 1:1, CEV)

Talk Point
God's creation is very good! God wants you to take care of God's world.

Items Needed
small stuffed animals, paper, crayons, affirmation stickers

God Talk
Give each child a stuffed animal to hold.

Our Bible tells us that God made a beautiful world. What are some of the things God made? *(stars, moon, sun, people, animals, sea, plants)* God wants us to care for God's world. How can we do this? *(take care of the animals, pick up trash, recycle)* How many of you have pets? How do you help care for your pets? *(feed my cat, walk my dog, change the hamster cage)* When you care for your pet, you are caring for the animals that God made. When you pick up trash or put trash in a garbage can rather than throwing it on the ground, you keep our world clean. When you recycle *(explain this term if children do not understand)* you help by using items over again rather than throwing them away. God is pleased when we take care of God's world.

Putting God Talk Into Action
Give each child a piece of paper and crayons. Encourage the children to draw pictures of God's world. Let each child share his or her drawing.

After sharing, give each child an affirmation sticker telling him or her that the picture is very good, just as God's creation is very good.

Prayer
Thank you, God, for your beautiful world. Help us to take good care of all that you made. Amen.

A Rainbow in the Sky

Bible Verse

When I send clouds over the earth, and a rainbow appears in the sky, I will remember my promise to you and to all other living creatures. Never again will I let floodwaters destroy all life.

(Genesis 9:14-15, CEV)

Talk Point

The rainbow is a sign of God's promise to all people and all the animals. God will never again destroy all of life on earth with a flood. This shows God love and care for all living things. This is God's promise to you.

Items Needed

plastic containers with lids, colored sand (red, orange, yellow, green, blue, and violet) or strips of colored paper (red, orange, yellow, green, blue, and violet), paper, glue

God Talk

Have you ever seen a rainbow in the sky after it has rained? *(Let the children respond and tell their own stories.)* God promises us that whenever we see a rainbow in the sky, God will never again destroy all the earth with a flood. This promise reminds us that God loves and cares for each of us. God also made this promise to the animals because God also loves the animals.

People sometimes make promises that they forget to keep. God always keeps God's promises. Whenever we see a rainbow in the sky we need to stop and thank God for God's wonderful promise.

The Bible tells us that Noah and his family were the only people alive who did what God wanted. Could you imagine a world in which only one family obeyed God and lived the way God wished? After the flood, God promised the people and animals that a flood would never destroy the entire world. Today we still have floods in some parts of the world, but never a flood greater than the one that we read about in the Bible.

When we see a rainbow in the sky we can remember God's promise. We can also remember how much God loves us.

Putting God Talk Into Action

Give each child a plastic container with a secure top. Have the children layer their sand in the container to represent the colors of the rainbow. Or give each child one strip of paper for each color of the rainbow and have them glue the strips on a piece of paper to represent the rainbow.

Prayer

Thank you, God, for the rainbow and your promise to all people and animals. Thank you for loving us. Amen.

God Is Our Good Shepherd

Bible Verse

You, LORD, are my shepherd. I will never be in need.
(Psalm 23:1, CEV)

Talk Point

Just as the shepherd cares for the sheep, God cares for you.

Items Needed

person dressed in costume as a shepherd holding a shepherd's crook, cookies in the shape of a shepherd's staff, cookie decorations

God Talk

Today we have a shepherd who is visiting with us. He brought along his shepherd's crook to show you the way he cares for his sheep. In Bible times, shepherds used their shepherd's crooks to protect the sheep from bears, lions, or other dangerous animals. They used the shepherd's crooks to hit the animals that tried to attack the sheep. They also used the shepherd's crooks to lead a sheep that tried to stray from the flock. The shepherd reached out with the crook and brought the stray animal safely back to the flock.

Let's pretend that you are sheep. Get down on your hands and knees and pretend that you are sheep in a flock together. *(Let the children make sheep-like noises. Select one child to be the sheep who strays from the flock. Have the shepherd gently use his crook to bring the sheep back to the flock. Continue to do this until all the children have the opportunity to play the role of the lost sheep.)*

The Bible tells us that God acts like a good shepherd. God guides us and directs us. God leads us in the right direction in our lives. God provides for our needs. God protects us.

Putting God Talk Into Action

Give the children two cookies to decorate. Explain to the children that the cookies are shaped like shepherds' crooks. As the children decorate their cookies, have the shepherd walk around and remind each child that God is his or her shepherd.

Let the children eat one of their decorated cookies and encourage them to give the other one to someone who has loved and protected them.

Prayer
Thank you, God, for caring for me like a shepherd cares for the sheep. Amen.

God Talk Reminder
Preschool children are not abstract thinkers. It will be difficult for them to make the transition from the shepherd to God as Shepherd. However, preschoolers will enjoy having the shepherd visit their class. They will understand that shepherds existed in Bible times and cared for their sheep. They will also realize that there are persons that care for them and offer them protection. They will learn that God cares for them and offers them protection, as do family members and friends.

Shepherd's Staff Cookies
3-oz pkg. soft cream cheese
½ cup soft margarine
½ cup firmly packed brown sugar
½ tsp vanilla
1⅔ cups flour

Mix together cream cheese, margarine, sugar, salt, and vanilla. Blend well. Add flour. Mix together until dough forms a ball. Knead the dough on a floured surface. Add more flour if dough is sticky.

Roll the dough into a ropelike shape. Place the dough on an ungreased cookie sheet. Curve one end into a shepherd's crook. Bake the cookies at 350 degrees for eight to ten minutes.

Flowers in a Field

Bible Verse
Why worry about clothes? Look how the wild flowers grow. They don't work hard to make their clothes. But I tell you that Solomon with all his wealth wasn't as well clothed as one of them.

(Matthew 6:28-29, CEV)

Talk Point
We do not have to worry. God takes care of us and provides for our needs.

Items Needed
craft sticks, cupcake papers, glue, pictures of wild flowers or real wild flowers

God Talk
Show the children a picture of wild flowers or some real wild flowers.

What are some things that you worry about? *(Let the children respond.)* Jesus tells us not to worry. Instead, Jesus tells us to look at the wild flowers growing in a field. These flowers do not have to worry about the clothes they wear. They are so beautiful because God made them. Jesus mentions a man by the name of Solomon. Solomon was a wealthy king who had expensive clothes to wear; yet Jesus tells us that the wild flowers are more beautiful than all of Solomon's clothes!

God takes care of us and provides for our needs. We do not have to worry. We can depend on God to help us. Worry only leads us away from God. Instead of worrying, God wants us to pray for help and ask advice from our parents, friends, and teachers. We should always share things that are bothering us or causing us worry with our parents.

Putting God Talk Into Action
Give each child a craft stick and a cupcake paper. Have him or her glue the cupcake paper to the craft stick to form a flower.

Prayer
Thank you, God, for the beautiful flowers. I do not have to worry. You will take care of me just as you take care of the wild flowers. Amen.

We Prepare for Baby Jesus (Advent)

Bible Verse

She gave birth to her firstborn child, a son, wrapped him snugly, and laid him in a manger, because there was no place for them in the guestroom.
(Luke 2:7, CEB)

Talk Point

The season of Advent is a special time in the church, a time when you and your family get ready for the birth of Christ.

Items Needed

green and purple foam sheets, paper punch, purple ribbon, baby items (baby blanket, shoes, socks, toys), glue, picture of candles (page 24), scissors

God Talk

Give each child a baby item to hold.

What are some of the ways a family prepares for the birth of a new baby? *(For children who do not have siblings, have them to think about a friend or relative who had a new addition to the family.)*

In our church and home, we celebrate a special time called *Advent*. We use the four Sundays before Christmas Day to get ready for the birth of Jesus.

During Advent we light four candles, one each Sunday before Christmas Day. The color for Advent is purple (or blue). Purple is the color for royalty, and we remember that Jesus is our King.

Before a baby is born, a family prepares for the birth. They buy baby items and prepare the baby's room. They think about what they will name the baby. In the same way, we prepare for the birth of Jesus by lighting our candles. Each time we light a candle; we remember that soon it will be Christmas Day, the day we celebrate the birth of Jesus. We take time to thank God for the gift of Jesus.

Putting God Talk Into Action

Punch two holes in the top of the green foam board and tie a purple ribbon through the holes so the children can hang their candles. Photocopy the candle pattern (below) for each child. Have each child use the pattern to cut four candles out of the purple foam sheet. (Precut the candles for the younger children.) Have the children glue their candles on the green foam, spacing apart each candle to represent the candles lit for the four Sundays of Advent.

Prayer

Advent is a special time in our church. Thank you, God, for sending Jesus into the world as a baby. Amen.

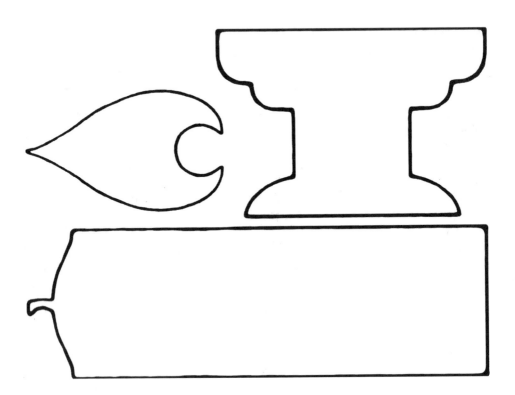

An Angel Visits Mary (Advent)

Bible Verse

Then Mary said, "I am the Lord's servant. Let it be with me just as you have said." Then the angel left her.

(Luke 1:38, CEB)

Talk Point

When an angel told Mary she was to give birth to Jesus, she believed the angel and accepted God's plan for her life. God has a plan for you.

Items Needed

craft sticks, ribbon, posterboard, glue, crayons or markers, stickers, scissors

God Talk

Mary was a teenage girl who lived in the village of Nazareth. One day an angel named Gabriel visited Mary. Angels are messengers from God. God had a special plan for Mary. God wanted Mary to give birth to Jesus. Gabriel told Mary God's plan.

How would you feel if an angel came to you with a message from God? *(Let the children respond.)* At first Mary was afraid. She could not understand why this was happening to her. The angel Gabriel told her that God had chosen her among all the women in the world. When Mary heard this she believed Gabriel and agreed to accept what God wanted her to do in her life.

God has a plan for our lives. How can we learn God's plan for our lives? Think about some of the things you are good at doing or things that you enjoy. *(Let the children respond by sharing things they are good at doing or things they enjoy.)* Think of the subjects in school you enjoy. *(Let the children respond by sharing subjects they like in school.)* Listen to friends and parents when they tell you that you are good at doing certain things. Pray each day that God will help you understand what God's plan for your life is, just as God showed Mary.

Putting God Talk Into Action

Give each child a piece of posterboard cut into a 4½- by 4½- inch square. Have the children write: "God has a plan for my life." in the middle part of the square. Let the children decorate around the words with crayons or markers and stickers. Give each child four craft sticks. Have the children glue their craft sticks around the edge of the square to make a frame. Attach a piece of ribbon for hanging.

Prayer

God, we are glad you had a plan for Mary's life. Your plan for her was to give birth to Jesus. We're glad you also have a plan for our lives. Help us to follow that plan. Amen.

God Talk Reminder

You will need to assist preschool children with the gluing of their frames. Photocopy the words below on the posterboard for each preschool child.

God
has a plan
for my life.

Angels Tell About the Birth of Jesus (Advent)

Bible Verse

Suddenly many other angels came down from heaven and joined in praising God. They said: "Praise God in heaven! Peace on earth to everyone who pleases God."

(Luke 2:13-14, CEV)

Talk Point

God sent angels to tell the good news of Jesus' birth. The angels offered praise to God. You can praise God and tell others about the birth of Jesus.

Items Needed

posterboard; scissors; glue; crayons; CD with the song "Angels We Have Heard on High"; CD player; angel figurine, angel pattern (page 29); crayons or markers

God Talk

Show the children an angel figurine.

Angels are messengers who tell people what God wants them to know. When Jesus was born, God sent angels to tell the good news of Jesus' birth to shepherds who were watching their sheep in the field outside the little town of Bethlehem. The Bible tells us that the shepherds were afraid when they first saw the angel, but the angel told them not to be afraid because there was great news. A baby had been born. This was not just any baby, however! This baby was Jesus, the Savior of the world.

Have you every received some great news? *(Let the children respond.)* How did you feel? *(Let the children respond.)* Can you imagine how joyful the shepherds were when they heard the good news that Jesus was born? We are also joyful today when we hear the story of the birth of Jesus.

The Bible tells us that the angels praised God—and you can too. You can praise God for the birth of Jesus. You can sing songs, clap your hands, and thank God for Jesus. You can tell others about the birth of Jesus just like the angels told the shepherds.

Listen to a song about the angels who appeared to the shepherds. This is a hymn that we sing in our church, "Angels We Have Heard on High." Follow my motions and do what I do as we listen to the music. As we do the motions, we remember to praise God for Jesus. (*Motions: clap hands, sway to music, march around the room, lift hands in the air, march in place, turn around in a circle, snap fingers, pat head, rub tummy.*)

Putting God Talk Into Action

Have the children trace their handprints on posterboard. Cut out the handprint and use these for angel wings.

Have the children trace the angel pattern (page 29) on posterboard and cut it out. (Help the younger children cut out their angels). Have the children glue their handprint wings to the back of the angel. Let the children use crayons or makers to add faces and hair on their angels.

Encourage the children to give their angels to friends or family members and tell them the story of the angels.

Prayer

Thank you, God, for sending angels to tell the shepherds about the birth of Jesus. Help us, like the angels, to praise you and to share with others the good news of Jesus' birth. Amen.

29

Shepherds Visit Baby Jesus (Advent)

Bible Verse

When the angels returned to heaven, the shepherds said to each other, "Let's go right now to Bethlehem and see what's happened." They went quickly and found Mary and Joseph, and the baby lying in a manger. The shepherds returned home, glorifying and praising God for all they had heard and seen.

(Luke 2:15-16, 20, CEB)

Talk Point

Like the shepherds, you can praise God.

Items Needed

cotton balls, glue, sheep pattern (page 31)

God Talk

At the time Jesus was born in Bethlehem, God sent angels to share the good news of Jesus' birth with shepherds. After the shepherds learned the news of Jesus' birth, they hurried to the stable and found Jesus lying on a bed of hay. They talked with Mary and Joseph, telling them about the visit of the angels. Then shepherds returned to care for their sheep. As they returned, they praised God, saying wonderful things about God.

Encourage the children to think of all the wonderful things they can say about God. Write these things on the board. *(Let the children respond.)*

Putting God Talk Into Action

Photocopy the sheep (page 31) for each child. Give each child several cotton balls. Each time you read out one of the wonderful things the children have said about God, have each child glue one cotton ball on his or her sheep. Continue until the sheep is covered with wool.

Prayer

Like the shepherds, we praise you, God, for your son, Jesus. Amen.

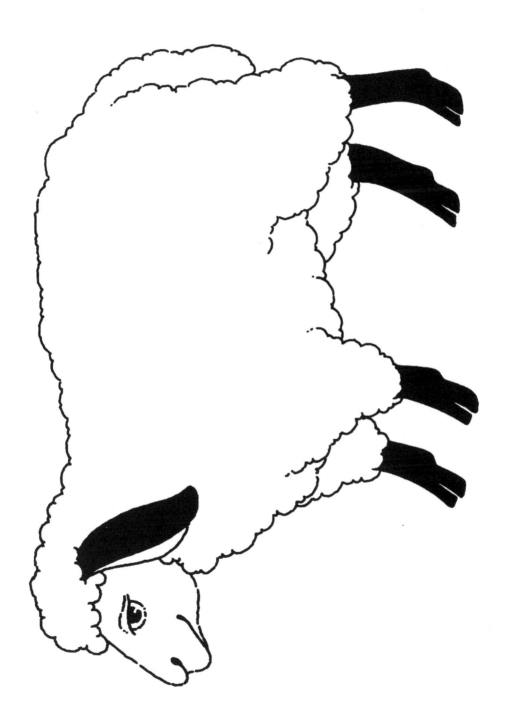

A Star Leads the Way (Epiphany)

Bible Verse

They were thrilled and excited to see the star.

(Matthew 2:10, CEV)

Talk Point

God guides you just as the star guided the wise men.

Items Needed

unbreakable star ornament, glitter, markers or crayons, paper punch, ribbon, scissors, star pattern (page 33)

God Talk

Hold up a star.

When Jesus was born, some wise men saw a bright, shining star in the sky. They followed the star to the house where Jesus stayed with his family. They brought presents to Jesus and worshiped him. The star guided the wise men.

God guides boys and girls today. Sometimes God uses people to help guide children. Think of some people who guide you today. Let's sit in a circle. *(Form a circle.)* I am going to play some music as you pass the star around the circle. When the music stops, whoever is holding the star will name someone who guides us today.

Continue around the circle until all of the children have the opportunity to name guides: parents, teachers, friends, pastors, and neighbors.

There is a special book that guides us. Can you think of the name of that book? *(the Bible)* The Bible guides us and helps us find Jesus.

Putting God Talk Into Action

Photocopy the star pattern (below) for each child. Cut out the star or let the children cut out their own stars. Encourage the children to decorate their stars with glitter, markers, or crayons. Punch a hole in the top of the star and help the children tie a ribbon for hanging.

Prayer

God, thank you for the star that guided the wise men to Jesus. Thank you for the people who guide us today. Thank you for the Bible, a special book that guides us. We are thankful that you guide our lives. Amen.

Palm Sunday Parade (Lent)

Bible Verse

The next day the great crowd that had come for the festival heard that Jesus was coming to Jerusalem. They took palm branches and went out to meet him. They shouted, "Hosanna! *Blessings on the one who comes in the name of the Lord! Blessings on the king of Israel!"* Jesus found a young donkey and sat on it, just as it is written, *Don't be afraid, Daughter Zion. Look! Your king is coming, sitting on a donkey's colt.*
(John 12:12-15, CEB)

Talk Point

Jesus entered Jerusalem riding on a donkey to show the people that he was the king of peace. The people praised Jesus by waving palm branches and shouting "hosanna." You can praise God today.

Items Needed

8-inch paper plates, leaf pattern (page 36), hosanna sign (page 36), felt flowers stickers, ribbon, picture of Palm Sunday scene, palm branches, crayons or markers, scissors

God Talk

Show the children the Palm Sunday picture and ask them to tell you what they know about the story. Read the story to the children in a Bible storybook or Children's Bible.

Have you ever been to a parade? *(Let the children share their experiences.)* Parades are fun events of celebration. When a parade takes place, people line the streets, laugh, clap, and are often very noisy! The Bible tells us the story of the time Jesus came into the city of Jerusalem riding on a donkey. You might think of a parade when you hear the story!

Jesus and his disciples traveled to Jerusalem for a special celebration for the Jewish people. They were going to celebrate the Passover, a time for the people to remember the story of when their ancestors were slaves in Egypt. Jesus got on a donkey and rode into the city. When the people saw him coming, they cut down palm branches and waved them. Some people took off their cloaks and put them down on the road as Jesus passed by on the donkey. The air was filled with excitement as the crowd shouted "hosanna," which means "help us" or "save us."

By riding into the city on a donkey, Jesus reminded the crowd that he was not going to be a mighty king, but a humble one. He wanted to be a king of peace, not a ruler of violence and hatred. Powerful kings rode on majestic horses, but Jesus rode on a donkey.

When the people spread their cloaks on the ground, they were showing honor and respect. Waving palm branches in Jesus' day was like our waving flags today. As the people waved palm branches and spread their cloaks on the ground, they also shouted "hosanna" because they believed Jesus could help them.

Jesus came to bring peace to the world. How can there be peace in our world today? (respect other people, work to end war, talk with our enemies) How can you be a peacemaker today? (not fight with my brother or sister, be kind to others, not bully others, get along with my friends, not argue with my parent)

Putting God Talk Into Action

Give each child a palm branch and lead him or her on a Palm Sunday processional. Let the children shout, "Hosanna" as they march.

Make a Palm Sunday wreath. Give each child an 8-inch paper plate. Have the children cut out the inside circle of the plate. (Precut the plates for the younger children.) Give each child several leaves that you have cut from the leaf pattern (page 36). Let the children color the leaves green. Give each child one of the signs that reads "hosanna" (page 36) and let the children color the signs. Let the children glue their leaves around the wreath. Give them some "peel off" felt flowers to add to the wreath. Have them glue their "hosanna sign" to the top of the wreath. Add a ribbon by gluing it to the back of the wreath for hanging.

Prayer

God, help us to be children of peace. Amen.

Hosanna

Jesus Turns Over the Tables in the Temple (Lent)

Bible Verse

Then Jesus went into the temple and threw out all those who were selling and buying there. He pushed over the tables used for currency exchange and the chairs of those who sold doves. He said to them, "It's written, *My house will be called a house of prayer.* But you've made it a hideout for crooks."

(Matthew 21:12-13, CEB)

Talk Point

Jesus turned over the tables in the Temple to teach us that we must respect God and care for our place of worship.

Items Needed

pieces of felt, small dowel rods, yarn, pictures of ways persons worship (page 39), play money coins, crayons, scissors

God Talk

Give the children a coin to hold while you share with them.

In New Testament times, people came to the Temple in Jerusalem to worship God. However, before they could worship they had to purchase a sacrifice. A sacrifice was an animal that was used as an offering to God.

Jesus was upset with those who were selling the animals because they cheated. The sellers charged more money than the animals were worth. Then the sellers kept the extra money for themselves.

Many people came to the Temple to worship from many different places. Often the people brought the kind of money they used in their countries.

 When they arrived at the Temple they needed to exchange their coins for Temple coins.

Jesus was not happy with the moneychangers who exchanged the foreign coins for the travelers. He knew that the moneychangers cheated. They gave the travelers less money for their coins than they were worth. Jesus called the moneychangers and the sellers robbers because they cheated the people and were not honest.

Jesus knew that the Temple should be a place of worship and prayer. Jesus taught the people to worship God in ways that please God.

Putting God Talk Into Action

Prepare a banner for each child. Glue or staple the dowel rod to the piece of felt. Tie a piece of yarn to the dowel rod for hanging.

Give each child a copy of the picture showing ways we worship God today (page 39). Let the children talk about each picture *(praying, exploring God's creation, singing, dancing, creating art, reading the Bible)*

Have the children color the pictures and cut them out. *(Cut out the pictures for the younger children.)* Let the children glue their pictures on their banners.

Prayer

God, Jesus taught us that our places of worship are important. We must show respect and love for you when we worship. Thank you for our church. Help us worship you in ways that please you. Amen.

Ways We Worship

Children Praise Jesus (Lent)

Bible Verse

The men said to Jesus, "Don't you hear what those children are saying?" "Yes, I do!" Jesus answered. "Don't you know that the Scriptures say, 'Children and infants will sing praises'?"

(Matthew 21:16, CEV)

Talk Point

Jesus was happy when the children praised God in the Temple. It is good when we praise and worship God.

Items Needed

sturdy paper plates, staples or glue, paper punch, chenille stems, musical instruments, jingle bells, crayons or markers or stickers, tape, scissors

God Talk

Take the children on a walking tour of the sanctuary. Stop at places where people sing praises to God. (choir loft, organ, piano, pews) *Give thanks and praise for the worship leader or leaders such as adult choir director, organist, pianist, adult handbell choir director, and those who lead the youth and children's choirs and children's handbell choirs. Offer thanks and praise for the members of the adult, youth, and children's choirs, members of the adult, youth, and children's handbell choirs, and commend the singing of the congregation during worship.*

Our Bible story takes place during the last week of Jesus' life. Jesus enters the Temple in Jerusalem and heals many people. The religious leaders criticize the children who praise Jesus because they believe the children are making too much noise! Jesus tells the religious leaders that the Scriptures allow for the praises of children. Jesus listened to the praise of children and was pleased. It's a good thing when children today sing praises to God or play musical instruments to worship God.

Putting God Talk Into Action

Pass out musical instruments and let the children play and sing some of their favorite Bible songs.

Let the children make tambourines. Ahead of time, staple or glue two sturdy paper plates together. If you choose to staple the plates, cover the staples with tape. Let the children decorate their tambourines with crayons, markers, or stickers.

Punch holes around the side of the plates for each child. Cut chenille stems in half. Give the children jingle bells and a chenille stem half for each of the holes. Help each child thread the jingle bells onto the chenille stems. Then thread the chenille stems through the holes. Twist the ends of each chenille stem together to secure the bell.

Have the children sing songs, march, and dance as they play their tambourines.

Prayer

God, help us to praise you with the same excitement as the children praised Jesus in the Temple. Amen.

God Talk Reminder

Adults will need to tie the jingle bells and punch holes for the younger children. Extra helpers are recommended for this project.

Jesus Shares a Special Meal With His Disciples (Lent)

Bible Verse

Jesus took some bread in his hands and gave thanks for it. He broke the bread and handed it to his apostles. Then he said, "This is my body, which is given for you. Eat this as a way of remembering me!"
(Luke 22:19, CEV)

Talk Point

Jesus shared a special meal with his disciples. We remember Jesus in our church when we share in our time of Holy Communion.

Items Needed

cloth, washable paint, shallow containers, sponges shaped in Christian symbols, paint smocks, hand-washing supplies, recycled newspapers

God Talk

Families and friends enjoy special meals together. What are some of the special meals you share with your family and friends? *(birthday celebrations, Thanksgiving, Christmas, guests invited to dinner)*

Jesus shared a special meal called the Passover with his disciples. The Passover meal remembered when the Jewish people were slaves in Egypt and Moses followed God's plan to free the people.

Our Bible story takes place during the last week of Jesus' life. Jesus and his disciples came together for the special Passover meal. During the meal, Jesus blessed the bread. He reminded the disciples that whenever they gathered to share this special meal, they were to remember him.

In our church we remember Jesus when we dip our bread into grape juice and eat the bread. *(Note: Share with the children about Communion according to your church's practice.)* We call this time Holy Communion. Our pastor invites everyone present to come and share in this special meal. Children are invited to participate because children are an important part of our church family. When we share in Holy Communion, we remember how much Jesus loves us and all of the people of the world.

Let's sing together, "Jesus Loves the Little Children."

Putting God Talk Into Practice

Let the children design a cloth for your church's Communion table. Give each child a paint smock to wear. Cover the table with recycled newspapers. Pour washable paint into shallow containers.

Show the children how to press their sponges in the paint and then to the cloth. Have the children wash their hands, or provide wipes. When the cloth is dry, let the children present it to the pastor.

Prayer

God, we are glad Jesus shared a special meal with his disciples. Jesus blessed the bread at the meal and told his disciples to always remember him. We want to remember Jesus. We remember Jesus in our church when our families share together in a special time called Holy Communion. We are happy we have a special time in our church to remember Jesus. Amen.

Jesus Washes His Disciples' Feet (Lent)

Bible Verse
Then he poured water into a washbasin and began to wash his disciples' feet, drying them with the towel he was wearing.

(John 13:5, CEB)

Talk Point
Jesus washed his disciples' feet to remind them that he came into the world to help others. Jesus wants you to learn how to help and care for others.

Items Needed
basin of water, towels, sponges, 9- by 12-inch pieces of white felt, yarn, paper punch, scissors, religious stamps, stamp pad

God Talk
Have an adult or youth play the role of Jesus. Have him dress in a biblical costume. Wear sandals or shoes that are easy to remove. As you talk, let Jesus wash your feet and dry them with a towel.

During the last meal that Jesus shared with his disciples, Jesus got up from the table, took a basin of water, and began to wash the dirty feet of his disciples. The disciples walked the roads wearing sandals and their feet got dusty and dirty. It was the custom during this time to have a slave wash the feet of travelers. A slave was not present in the room on the night Jesus shared a meal with his disciples, so Jesus did the washing! Imagine the surprise of the disciples when Jesus washed their feet and dried them with a towel.

After Jesus washed all of the disciples' feet, he began to talk with them about what he had done. He washed their feet to remind them to care for others in a humble way. A person could not act selfish or proud, but must show love and respect at all times. Doing good deeds for others is not an easy task, but you please God when you cheerfully and gladly help others.

Putting God Talk Into Action

Provide a basin of water, sponges, and towels. Let the children select a partner. Take turns washing one another's feet (or hands) and drying them with the towel.

Encourage the children to think of all of the chores or work at home and school they are required to do. Tell them to think especially of the ones they do not particularly enjoy or find difficult to perform. *(Give the children time to respond.)* Remind the children that they are helping others when they complete their chores or schoolwork. Encourage them to approach their chores or schoolwork cheerfully even when these tasks are difficult.

Make Action Aprons. Give each child a piece of white felt and a 4-foot length of yarn. Use the paper punch to make holes (about 2 inches apart) across one longer side of each piece of felt. Show the children how to lace yarn through the holes, creating apron "strings." Let them wear their aprons to clean up their church classroom or room at home.

Prayer

Thank you, God, that Jesus washed his disciples' feet to teach them and us how to help others. Show us how to help others in a way that pleases you. Amen.

God Talk Reminder

It will be difficult for preschool and younger children to make the leap from Jesus' washing of the disciples' feet to the concept of humility and servanthood. Use the story to talk about doing good deeds for others just as Jesus did a good deed for his disciples. Let the children see the task of washing feet as hard work, just as they sometimes have to perform hard work at school or home. Guide them to develop an attitude like that of Jesus, one of caring, love, and joy, even when the task at hand is difficult.

Jesus Dies on the Cross
(Lent)

Bible Verse

Jesus shouted, "Father, I put myself in your hands!" Then he died.
(Luke 23:46, CEV)

Talk Point

Jesus died on the cross. He trusted God even when he was dying. You can trust God each moment of your life. You can trust God in life and in death. God is always with you.

Items Needed

various styles or shapes of crosses, black construction paper, white paper, outer and inner church window pattern (page 48), cross pattern (page 48), markers or crayons, glue, small pocket crosses, scissors

God Talk

Show the children the various styles and shapes of crosses. Let the children point out any crosses in the sanctuary. Ask the children if any of them are wearing crosses.

The cross reminds us of the way Jesus died. The cross also reminds us that we are followers of Jesus.

Our Bible story today is a sad one for the followers of Jesus. Some people did not understand that Jesus was God's Son. They failed to understand that Jesus came to earth to teach people about God and show God's love. Some people convinced the rulers in charge to arrest Jesus. After his arrest, Jesus was sentenced to die on a cross. The Roman government ruled the land at the time of Jesus. Crucifixion (killing a person on a cross) was one of the cruel ways the Roman government put people to death. Dying on a cross was a terrible way to die. We are sad today when we think about Jesus dying on the cross. Yet, even on the cross Jesus forgave the very people who put him to death.

As Jesus was dying on the cross, he trusted in God. Jesus trusted in God from the time he was born to the day he died. You can trust God all of your life. God will always be with you.

When you wear a cross or carry a cross today, you tell others that you are a follower or disciple of Jesus. *(Give the children small pocket crosses to carry with them.)*

Putting God Talk Into Action

Make a stained glass window cross. Photocopy the window pattern (page 48). Show the children how to separate and cut out the outer church window pattern, the inner church window pattern, and the cross. (Precut the patterns for the younger children.)

Have the children trace the outer window pattern and the cross pattern on black construction paper, and the inner church window pattern on white paper. Have the children cut out each pattern. (Precut the patterns for the younger children.)

Show the children how to fold their white window shapes at different angles. Make sure to crease each fold. Tell the children to keeping folding and unfolding their paper until they can see the patterns they have made.

Have the children unfold their paper and trace the creased lines with dark markers. Let the children glue the inner windows onto the outer windows.

Encourage the children to color the different shapes with markers or crayons. Instruct each child to glue the black cross in the middle of the window.

Prayer

Thank you, God, that Jesus trusted you in life and in death. Help us to always trust you. Amen.

God Talk Reminder

It is difficult for children to understand the theological concept of Christ dying on the cross for our sins. Be prepared to answer difficult questions older children may ask. Consult your pastor if you need help explaining Christ's death.

Jesus Is Alive! (Easter)

Bible Verse

Why are you looking in the place of the dead for someone who is alive?
Jesus isn't here! He has been raised from death.

(Luke 24:5-6, CEV)

Talk Point

The good news of Easter is that Jesus is alive!

Items Needed

foam trays, moss (from craft stores), small stones, plastic eggs, small twigs, yarn, play dough

God Talk

Recruit a woman to dress in biblical costume and portray one of the women who discovered the empty tomb. Have her wait outside your meeting space during your initial explantation.

After Jesus died on the cross, he was buried in a tomb. On Sunday morning, some women who were followers of Jesus came to the tomb to anoint Jesus' body with spices. It was the custom during that time to put spices on a person who had died. As the women approached the tomb, they were very surprised to find the huge stone rolled away. They were even more surprised when they did not find Jesus' body inside the tomb. Instead, they found two angels. The angels told them the good news that Jesus was not in the tomb. Jesus was alive!

Have the woman enter, shouting, "Jesus is alive!" several times. Have the children shout with her. Have the woman exit, still shouting.

Give each children an empty plastic egg. Open up your plastic egg. What do you find inside? *(Give the children time to respond.)* There is nothing inside your plastic egg, is there? Your plastic egg is empty to help you remember that Jesus' tomb was empty. Jesus was not there.

When the women discovered that the tomb was empty, they hurried to share the good news with the disciples of Jesus. At first, the disciples did not believe the women. Later on, however, they believed the good news and celebrated with the women. Jesus was alive! Like the women, you can share the good news with others that Jesus is alive!

Putting God Talk Into Action

Make an Easter garden. Give each child a foam tray, moss, and a few stones. Have the child place the moss in the tray and add the stones to form steps toward the empty tomb. Have the child place the empty tomb (*plastic egg opened up slightly*) beside the stone pathway.

Give each child two small twigs and show them how to tie their twigs together with yarn to make a cross. Place the cross inside the garden using a small piece of play dough as a stand.

Prayer

Thank you, God, for Easter. Thank you for raising Jesus from the dead. Jesus is alive! Help us to share the good news like the women shared with others. Amen.

Happy Birthday, Church! (Pentecost)

Bible Verse
The Holy Spirit took control of everyone, and they began speaking whatever languages the Spirit let them speak.
(Acts 2:4, CEV)

Talk Point
The Holy Spirit came at Pentecost. Pentecost celebrates the birthday of the church. The Holy Spirit is present today and helps you.

Item Needed
foam, foam shapes, yarn, pinwheels, scissors

God Talk
Today we celebrate a special day in our church. We call this day Pentecost. The Bible tells us that on Pentecost, a Jewish day of celebration, God sent the Holy Spirit into a room where many of Jesus' friends were gathered. The people began to speak in new languages and the people who knew those languages understood what the others were saying. It was a wonderful day! The coming of the Holy Spirit reminded the people that Jesus was always with them. After the coming of the Holy Spirit, people began to start churches so everyone could worship Jesus. This is why we call Pentecost the birthday of the church.

Today the Holy Spirit helps you in many ways. The Holy Spirit is present when you are sad. The Holy Spirit guides you so that you know what is right and what is wrong. The Holy Spirit helps you make your decisions. The Holy Spirit corrects you when you have not obeyed God. The Holy Spirit leads you to follow God's commandments. The Holy Spirit is present with you at all times and in all places.

In the Bible, in the Book of Acts, the Holy Spirit is described as "wind." We cannot see the wind, but we can certainly feel the power of the wind as it blows.

Putting God Talk Into Action

Give the children pinwheels. Let them go outside and watch their pinwheels blow in the wind. Remind them that we can feel the presence of the Holy Spirit even if we cannot see the Holy Spirit.

Give the children a piece of foam. Show them how to cut around in a spiral until they get to the middle of the circle. Decorate the spiral with foam shapes. Let each child attach a piece of yarn to the spiral shape so it can be hung. This craft can remind the children that the Holy Spirit is present even though they cannot see the Holy Spirit.

Celebrate the birthday of the church. Give the children party hats and blowers. Serve cupcakes and sing Happy Birthday to the church.

Prayer

Thank you, God, for the Holy Spirit. Amen.

God Talk Reminder

Preschoolers will not be able to cut out the spiral foam piece. Precut the spirals and let the children decorate them.

God Changes Me

Bible Verse

Don't be like the people of this world, but let God change the way you think. Then you will know how to do everything that is good and pleasing to him.

(Romans 12:2, CEV)

Talk Point

God can change (transform) you into a child that is good and pleasing to God.

Item Needed

Transformer® toy, capsule sponge dissolve toys, bowls of warm water

God Talk

Have one child who is good at working with a Transformer® toy demonstrate to the other children the way the toy changes from one shape to another. Point out the change in the toy.

Paul, the man who wrote the book of Romans in our Bible, tells us that God wants to change us into boys and girls that are good and pleasing to God. Paul tells us not to be like the people of this world who do not wish to obey God and who do not want to be changed. Paul advises us to let God change the way we think. God desires you to think about good things; things that help you grow in ways that please God.

Today we saw our transformer change from a _____ to a _____. We did not have to add any parts to our transformer in order for it to change. We simply worked with the parts we had. We turned and twisted the pieces of our transformer until it was changed into a new shape. Another word we use for change is *transform*. God works with you using all of your parts that God made. God works patiently and lovingly to change your parts and make all of them pleasing to God.

God wants to take all of your parts — your minds, your bodies, and your hearts — and change (transform) them in order to please God. You must be willing to let God transform you.

Putting God Talk Into Action

Give each child a capsule sponge dissolve toy. Provide bowls of warm water. Let the children drop their capsule sponge dissolve toys into the warm water and watch them dissolve and change into new shapes. Let the children take their sponge shapes home with them.

Prayer

Thank you, God, for working each day to change, transform, and shape each of us into a new and better person. Amen.

God Talk Reminder

For safety reasons, carefully watch all children, especially preschoolers, to avoid swallowing the capsule. If you are concerned about this, drop the capsule into the water for each child individually.

God Is Light

Bible Verse

God is light and there is no darkness in him at all.

(1 John 1:5, CEB)

Talk Point

God's love shines at all times and in all places of our world. God wants me to show God's love to others.

Items Needed

baby food jars, tea candles, markers, ribbon, Bible verse (page 56), glue, matches or lighter (for adult use only), scissors

God Talk

Have you ever had the lights go out at your home at night due to a storm? *(Let the children respond.)* Your family probably lit some candles or used flashlights to see in the dark until the light came back on in your house. Do you remember what it felt like when the lights finally came back on? Everyone was happy because without the light you could not see.

The Bible tells us that God is light and does not have any darkness. God's love never grows dim or goes away from us. God's love always shines brightly. God brings the light of love to places in our world where people need God's love to shine. *(Mention some recent event in the world or community where persons need God's light to shine.)* Today there are many places where people are hungry, sick, sad, lonely, afraid, or hurting. God expects you and me to help. When you care for others and show kindness, you help God's love to shine for people in need. *(You might mention some service projects your church or family has recently done to help others in need.)*

When the light went out in your house, you were left in the dark until you were able to light a candle or use your flashlight. Even then you could not see very well until the lights came back on in your home. Isn't it wonderful to know today that God's love shines so brightly for each of us? God's love shines so brightly that you can know God is with you always, even when the lights go out!

Putting God Talk Into Action

Have several unlit candles in candleholders and place them where children cannot reach them. Teach the children the Bible verse, "God is light and there is no darkness in him at all." Let the children say this verse several times. As the children say the verse of Scripture, light a candle. Let the children continue to say the memory verse until all of the candles in the room are lit.

Photocopy and cut out the Bible verse (below) for each child. Have the children decorate the Bible verses with markers.

Give each child a baby food jar. Show the child how to glue the Bible verse around the jar. Tie a ribbon around the top of the jar. Place a tea candle inside.

Encourage the children to give their candles to special friends who are in need of the light of God. Remind them to tell their friends as they present their gifts that "God is light and there is no darkness in him at all."

Prayer

Thank you, God, that you are light. Help us to show your love to others. Amen.

God Talk Reminder

Younger children will find it difficult to understand the concept of God as light. Emphasize that God is love and God's love shines everywhere and at all times. Let preschool children memorize a shorter verse, "God is light."

God is light

Keep on Growing

Bible Verse

Let the wonderful kindness and the understanding that come from our Lord and Savior Jesus Christ help you to keep on growing.

(2 Peter 3:18, CEV)

Talk Point

You grow in your faith when you follow Jesus. You keep on growing when you study the Bible, pray, and help others. Jesus helps you grow.

Items Needed

small clay flower pots, potting soil, seeds, markers or stickers, picture of a person as a baby and picture of that same person at a different age

God Talk

Show the children the picture of the baby and the same individual who is now older. Talk about the ways that person has changed over the years.

You are growing and changing. Growing takes time, doesn't it? A baby cannot walk or talk when he or she is born. Parents must be patient and wait until it is the right time for their child to take their first steps or say their first words. You have changed a lot since you were a baby. You have grown in height, weight, language, and knowledge. You are learning new things each day that you live. Growing and learning takes time and patience.

In the same way, you are learning and growing in your faith. You are learning new things about God and Jesus as you study your Bible, listen to your Sunday school teachers, and ask questions of your parents, friends, and pastors. You are growing in your faith when you pray to God and attend worship, Sunday school, and other activities that help children learn about God and Jesus.

This is an exciting time in your life! The writer of 2 Peter tells us that Jesus understands all of the changes you are going through and that Jesus shows kindness to you as you grow physically and spiritually. Knowing that Jesus always extends understanding and kindness to you helps you grow in your faith in a positive and special way.

Putting God Talk Into Action

Give each child a small clay flowerpot. Encourage the children to decorate the outside of the flowerpots using markers or stickers.

Help each child add a small amount of potting soil to the flowerpot. Give the child flower seeds to put on top of the potting soil. Add potting soil on top of the seeds.

Tell the children to water their seeds and watch them grow into beautiful flowers. Remind them to show patience as they watch the seeds grow. Remind them to be patient as they experience their own growth.

Prayer

Thank you, Jesus, for showing us kindness and understanding as we grow. Amen.

Jesus Blesses Children

Bible Verse

Some people brought children to Jesus so that he would place his hands on them and pray. But the disciples scolded them. "Allow the children to come to me," Jesus said.

(Matthew 19:13-14, CEB)

Talk Point

Children were special to Jesus. He blessed children and prayed for them. You are special to Jesus!

Item Needed

picture of biblical scene of Jesus and the children, 9-by-12 sheets of posterboard, small mirrors, glue, markers

God Talk

Show the children the picture of Jesus blessing the children.

One day some parents brought their children to Jesus. They wanted Jesus to bless their children and pray with them. A blessing is a special way of showing someone they are important and special. The person offering a blessing places his or her hands upon the head of the person being blessed and says a special prayer.

Jesus' disciples thought that Jesus was too busy to take the time to bless the children. They told the parents to stop bothering Jesus. However, Jesus said to allow the children to come to him. Jesus believed that children were important. Jesus loved children and took time to talk and pray with them.

Think of the people who bless you today because they love and care for you. Name some of these people. *(parents, teachers, friends, pastors)*

All of these people think that you are very special. They bless you when they take time to listen to what you have to say. They bless you when they teach you lessons about God and Jesus. They bless you when they care for your needs and help you with any problems. You are very blessed! You are special to Jesus. You are just as important as the children Jesus blessed.

Putting God Talk Into Action

Give each child a piece of posterboard folded in half. Have the children write: "Who is special to Jesus?" on the front of the card. Encourage the children to decorate around the words.

Glue a small mirror on the inside of the card for each child. When the children open the card they will remember that they are special to Jesus.

Prayer

Thank you, God, that Jesus took time to bless and pray with children. Help us always remember that we are special to Jesus. Jesus loves children! Jesus loves all the children around the world. Amen.

Care for Others

Bible Verse
Be happy with those who are happy, and cry with those who are crying.
(Romans 12:15, CEB)

Talk Point
The Bible teaches you to rejoice with others when they are happy, but to comfort them when they are sad.

Items Needed
smiley face and sad face (page 63) puppets, reproducible gift tag (page 62), tape, resealable plastic bags, Hershey Hugs® candy, praying hand stickers, Bible stickers, adhesive bandages, scissors

God Talk
Photocopy the smiley face and sad face puppet (page 63) for each child. Fold the puppet along the dotted line. Tape the sides together. The smiley face will be on one side of the puppet, the sad face will be on the other side of the puppet. Give each child a puppet to hold while you talk. Show the child how to put a hand inside the puppet.

Paul teaches us in the book of Romans that we are to care for others. We are to go out of our way to watch when people are sad and when they are happy. If they are sad, we are to be sad with them. If they are happy, we are to be happy with them. We are to care for others at all times.

I am going to name some things that people may face in life. If you think this is a sad time for people, turn your sad face toward me. If you think the person is happy, turn your smiley face toward me.
A woman loses her job. *(sad face)*
A child makes a good grade on a test. *(smiley face)*
A person has a family member die. *(sad face)*
A child goes hungry because his family does not have money to buy food. *(sad face)*
A child has a birthday party. *(smiley face)*
A man lives on the streets because he has no home. *(sad face)*
A friend finds out that he or she has cancer. *(sad face)*

Remember to reach out and care for people when they are sad or when they are happy.

Putting God Talk Into Action

Photocopy and cut out the gift tag (below) for each child. Give each child a resealable plastic bag. Let the children decorate the bags with stickers.

Have the children place items inside the bag along with the gift tag. Talk to the children about each item.

Hershey Hugs® candy – We all need hugs.
Prayer sticker – I am praying for you.
Bible sticker – God's Word helps us in our time of need.
Adhesive bandages – We all need love, care, and protection when we are hurt.

Encourage each child to give the bag to someone who is sad and explain to that person what each item means.

Prayer

God, help us to care for others. Let us notice when others are sad, and let us pay attention when others are happy. Amen.

God Talk Reminder

Preschool children will have a difficult time explaining the meaning of the items in their bags. Just encourage them to give their gift to persons who are sad.

Hershey Hugs® candy – We all need hugs.
Prayer sticker – I am praying for you.
Bible sticker – God's Word helps us in our time of need.
Adhesive bandages – We all need love when we are hurt.

How to Treat Others

Bible Verse
Treat people in the same way you want people to treat you.

(Matthew 7:12, CEB)

Talk Point
Jesus wants you to treat others in the same way you wish to be treated.

Items Needed
white foam board, ribbon, paper punch, circle stickers, markers, Golden Rule rulers

God Talk

Purchase rulers with the Golden Rule written on them. Give each child a ruler.

Our Bible verse is known as the Golden Rule. We call it the Golden Rule because it is a valuable teaching of Jesus that is worth following in all of our relationships. Jesus taught us to treat other people in the same way we want them to treat us. If we want others to show kindness to us, we have to be kind to them. If we want others to respect us, we have to show them respect. If we want others to love us, we have to love them. Sometimes this is not easy, but we have to ask ourselves if we would want to be treated in an unkind and disrespectful manner.

Let's think about some of the ways children might treat others. Do a "thumbs-up" if this is the way God wants us to treat others. Do a "thumbs-down" if this is not the way God wants us to treat others.

Say the following statements for the children. Have the children respond with thumbs up or thumbs down.

Pushing another child. *(thumbs down)*
Taking another child's toy away. *(thumbs down)*
Sharing your toys. *(thumbs up)*
Helping your dad clean up from dinner. *(thumbs up)*
Reading to your younger brother. *(thumbs up)*

When you treat others the way God wants you to, others learn about God's love. You set an example for them of the way God want all of us to act and the words God wants all of us to say. They, in turn, will learn from you ways to please God. The world will become a much better place to live when you practice the Golden Rule.

Putting God Talk Into Action

Give each child a piece of white foam board. Punch two holes in the top of the foam board and attach a ribbon for hanging. Have the children write: "Treat people in the same way you want people to treat you." on the felt, leaving out the letter o in all of the words. Have the children place a circle sticker in place of the letter o.

Prayer

God, help us to follow the Golden Rule. Amen.

God Talk Reminder

Photocopy the Golden Rule (below) for preschool children and let them place circle stickers in place of the letter o.

Treat pe ple in the same way y u want pe ple t treat y u.

(Matthew 7:12, CEB)

Go and Tell About Jesus

Bible Verse
Go to the people of all nations and make them my disciples.
(Matthew 28:19, CEV)

Talk Point
Jesus taught us to go and tell others about him.

Items Needed
traffic signal (page 68), black, green, yellow, red construction paper, glue, scissors, Bible verse card (page 67), scissors

God Talk

Photocopy and cut out the traffic signal pattern (page 68). Use markers to add the red, yellow, and green to the circles to make the lights. Show the children the traffic signal.

What does the green light on a traffic signal tell the driver to do when it is lit up? *(The driver may go.)*

Today we have a verse of Scripture in the Bible that tells us to go and tell others the good news of Jesus. This teaching is called the *Great Commission.* Jesus wanted his followers to realize how important it was to share the good news about him with all the people of the world. Today we have missionaries who go into many countries of the world to teach others about Jesus. However, we do not have to be a missionary to tell others about Jesus. You can tell others about Jesus in the places you go each day.

What does the yellow light on our traffic signal tell the driver to do when it is lit up? *(The driver needs to slow down and get ready to stop because the light is about to change to red.)*

Just like the yellow light tells the driver to slow down, God wants us to slow down to take time to read our Bible, to pray, and to learn all we can about God and Jesus.

What does the red light on our traffic signal tell the driver to do when it is lit up? *(The driver must stop.)*

God wants you to stop, listen and obey God. God wants you to stop and listen to others who teach you. God wants you to stop and rest when you are tired. God wants you to come to church and worship. Then, you will be ready to go and tell others about Jesus!

Putting God Talk Into Action

Photocopy the traffic signal (page 68) and the circle for each child. Have the child cut out the signal, trace it onto black construction paper, and then cut it out. *(Precut the traffic signal for younger children.)* Have the child cut out the circle, trace it onto green, yellow, and red construction paper, and cut the circles out.

Instruct the children to glue their green, yellow and red circles onto the traffic signals in the correct order. Tell them to write the word GO on the green circle.

Photocopy and cut out the Bible verse (below) for each child. Let the children glue the verses on the backs of the traffic signals.

Prayer

Help us to share with others the good news about Jesus. Amen.

God Talk Reminder

Younger children may not connect the traffic signal to the Great Commission, but they will understand go, slow down, and stop.

Go to the people of all nations and make them my disciples. **(Matthew 28:19, CEV)**	**Go to the people of all nations and make them my disciples.** **(Matthew 28:19, CEV)**

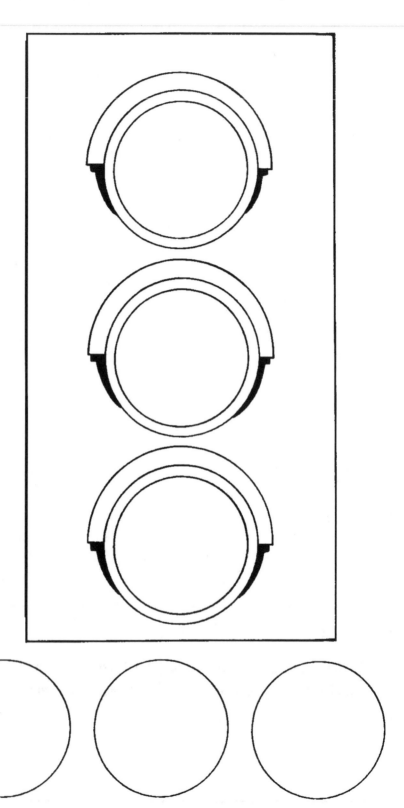

Jesus Eats in the Home of Zacchaeus

Bible Verse

When Jesus came to that spot, he looked up and said, "Zacchaeus, come down at once. I must stay in your home today." So Zacchaeus came down at once, happy to welcome Jesus.

(Luke 19:5-6, CEB)

Talk Point

When Zacchaeus met Jesus, he was changed forever. You are changed when you know Jesus. Zacchaeus welcomed Jesus into his home. You are invited by Jesus to welcome him into your life.

Items Needed

children's Bible, paper plates, food magazines, scissors, glue, tree pattern (page 71), pencils, crayons, or markers

God Talk

Read the children the story of Zacchaeus from a children's Bible or tell them the story.

Jesus asked Zacchaeus to let him come into his home. I wonder what Zacchaeus served Jesus for dinner? The Bible does not tell us, but the Bible does tell us a part of the conversation between Zacchaeus and Jesus. Jesus knew that Zacchaeus was a tax collector and that he had robbed the people when he collected their taxes. He collected more money than was required and took the extra money and kept it. He cheated these people and as a result they did not have enough money to properly care for their own families.

During their time together, Zacchaeus stood up and promised Jesus that he would no longer cheat. Not only this, but he told Jesus he planned to give half of his property to the poor. Additionally, he decided to pay back four times more money to the people he cheated. Jesus praised Zacchaeus for his actions.

Encountering Jesus proves to be a life-changing experience for all of us. Jesus goes with you wherever you go. Jesus remains with you at all times. Jesus is with you in your house, your school, and at your sporting events. Jesus wants to change you like he changed Zacchaeus. Think about what needs to different in your life. Pray about this and let Jesus change you into a better person. If Jesus could change Zacchaeus, Jesus can change you! Remember, though, that Zacchaeus had to be willing to change and had to take actions that made his life better. You have to be willing to change as well and do whatever is necessary to make changes in your life to please Jesus.

Putting God Talk Into Action

Photocopy the tree pattern (page 71) for each child. Encourage the children to write down some things that need to be changed in their lives. You might give some suggestions such as: I need to improve my temper. I need to do my chores without complaining. I need to do my homework. I need to improve my grades. I need to help my mom at home. I need to treat my sister nicer. Tell the children to take their trees with them and pray each day about the changes they need to make in their lives.

Give each child a paper plate. Let him or her think about what meal they would serve Jesus if Jesus came to the child's home for dinner. Let the children look through the food magazines and cut out pictures of the food items they would serve. Have the children glue these pictures on their plates and share with the class about their special meal for Jesus.

Sing "Zacchaeus Was a Wee Little Man," using hand motions.

Prayer

Thank you, Jesus, for changing Zacchaeus into a better person and thank you for changing us into better persons. Amen.

God Talk Reminder

Younger children can simply color the picture of the tree.

Jesus Chooses Disciples

Bible Verse

During that time, Jesus went out to the mountain to pray, and he prayed to God all night long. At daybreak, he called together his disciples. He chose twelve of them whom he called apostles: Simon, whom he named Peter; his brother Andrew; James; John; Philip; Bartholomew; Matthew; Thomas; James the son of Alphaeus; Simon, who was called a zealot; Judas the son of James; and Judas Iscariot, who became a traitor.
(Luke 6:12-16, CEB)

Talk Point

Jesus called disciples to help him. You are a disciple of Jesus.

Items Needed

egg cartons, disciples names (page 73), stickers

God Talk

Jesus chose twelve men to help him with his work. These men are called apostles or disciples. They were his special helpers.

You are also a disciple of Jesus. Today, a disciple of Jesus is anyone who believes in Jesus, obeys Jesus, loves Jesus, and wants to follow his teachings.

Name the disciples as they are listed in the Bible. Then say the name of each child and say: "(Name of child) is a disciple of Jesus."

Putting God Talk Into Action

Give each child an egg carton. Let the children decorate the outside of their egg cartons with stickers.

Photocopy the names of the disciples (page 71) for each child. Have the children cut out the names of each disciple and place one of the names in each of the twelve holders in the egg carton. Encourage the children to memorize the names of the twelve disciples.

Prayer

Thank you, Jesus, that we are your disciples. Amen.

God Talk Reminder

Cut out the names of the disciples for the younger children ahead of time.

Simon Peter	Matthew
Andrew	Thomas
James	James, son of Alphaeus
John	Simon the zealot
Philip	Judas the son of James
Bartholomew	Judas Iscariot

Kind Words

Bible Verse

A kind answer soothes angry feelings, but harsh words stir them up.
(Proverbs 15:1, CEV)

Talk Point

Using kind words helps calm an angry person, but mean words only make that person angrier. God wants you to use kind words.

Items Needed

two large Styrofoam boards, paint stirrers, 5-by-7 pieces of posterboard, masking tape, paper plates, arrow (page 75), brads, rulers, fine-line markers, pencils, scissors

God Talk

Prior to God Talk, use a marker to write the word KIND on a plastic foam board and the word UNKIND on a second plastic foam board. List kind and unkind phrases individually on separate pieces of posterboard. Make the phrases into signs by taping a paint stirrer vertically to the back of each posterboard sheet.

Kind phrases: I love you. You are pretty. You are handsome. Please. You are nice. Excellent work. I am sorry. Thank you. I like you.

Unkind phrases: I hate you. You are stupid. You look ugly. You are bad. I don't like you. You bother me. You are a pest.

Hand out signs to the children. Place the foam boards in front of the children.

Have you ever encountered someone who was really angry with you, but the kinds words you used helped to calm that person down? We learn from the Bible that kind words have a good effect on an angry person, but harsh, unkind words make that person angrier. Let's look at some kind and unkind phrases. They are on the signs that you are holding.

Have each child read aloud his or her sign and decide whether it is a kind phrase or an unkind phrase. Stick the kind signs in the plastic foam board marked KIND and the unkind signs in the plastic foam board marked UNKIND.

God asks us to use kind words when we talk with each other. Kind words helps us feel better about ourselves. Unkind words can destroy our self-worth. When we find ourselves in situations where persons are angry with us, we are tempted to use angry words. Yet, God reminds us to think before we speak. Even if the person is still angry with you, your kind words helps make the situation better and erases some of the hurt and harm.

Putting God Talk Into Action

Give each child a paper plate. Have the children use rulers and pencils to divide their plates into sections. Let them take fine-line markers and trace over the pencil lines. Have the children write at the top of each plate section the name of a person with whom they need to share kind words.

Give each child a copy of the arrow (below), let him or her trace it on posterboard and cut it out. Help the children attach the arrows to the middles of their plates using brads, one for each child.

Encourage each child to spin the arrow each morning and see whose name the spinner points toward. The name it lands on should be the person the child tries to share a kind word with on that day.

Prayer

God, help us to use kind words even when we are angry. Amen.

God Talk Reminder

Cut out the arrow for preschool and younger children.

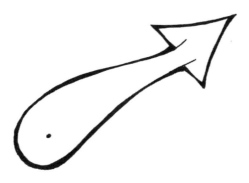

Encourage Each Other

Bible Verse
We should keep on encouraging each other to be thoughtful and to do helpful things.

(Hebrews 10:24, CEV)

Talk Point
God wants you to keep encouraging others. The Bible teaches you to be thoughtful and helpful and to remind others to do the same.

Items Needed
paper towel tubes, stickers

God Talk
Begin by saying encouraging words to each child by name.

When we love God, we want to encourage others. To encourage others, we say words that remind the person that he and she is a special child of God.

Our friends often get discouraged when they face problems in life that are difficult. They get worried when they do not think they are able to do what God wants them to do. They begin to put themselves down and believe that they are not valuable, especially if they are not encouraged. Sometimes they decide that no one cares about what is happening to them. You can offer encouragement to these friends. You can encourage them to do their very best and not to worry. You can tell them that God is always with them. You can remind them that Jesus loves them, and God will help them to use their gifts. You can do thoughtful acts of kindness to cheer others who are sad or lonely. You can do helpful things to let another person know that you care about him or her.

When you perform these good deeds, others realize that they, too, need to reach out to others and share God's love. Friends will follow your loving actions.

Putting God Talk Into Action

Make a whispering tube. Give each child a paper towel roll and let him or her decorate the roll with stickers.

Have each child whisper an encouraging word to another friend using the whispering tube. Suggest ideas for children to whisper such as: You are a good friend. You sing well. You serve as an acolyte. You are a good artist. You have a good sense of humor. You are very smart. You are a nice friend. You are very sweet.

Repeat this exercise several times so children can speak encouraging words to different friends.

Prayer

Thank you, God, for the encouraging words of friends. Help us to speak encouraging words to others. Help us to encourage others to share acts of kindness and find ways to help others. Amen.

Never Stop Praying

Bible Verse

Never stop praying, especially for others.

(Ephesians 6:18, CEV)

Talk Point

God never wants you to stop praying, especially for others.

Items Needed

cardboard chest or box, peel-off jewels, small slips of paper, pencils

God Talk

There are many ways to pray. Let me show you some of these ways. We can pray on our knees. *(Demonstrate and have the children to follow your actions.)* We can pray with our hands lifted into the air. *(Demonstrate and have the children to follow your actions.)* We can pray with our hands together. *(Demonstrate and have the children to follow your actions.)* We can pray with our hands crossed over our chest. *(Demonstrate and have the children to follow your actions.)*

God does not mind how you pray, but God does care if you pray. God wants you to pray each day. You can pray before you eat your meals. You can pray in the morning before you go to school. You can pray silently before a test at school. You can pray at night. You can pray when you have something hard you must do. You can pray to offer thanks to God. You can pray anytime! God hears your prayers.

God likes it very much when you take the time to pray for other people. Your prayers are ways to let your friends, family, or church members know that you care about them.

Prayer is very important. Prayer allows you to tell God, in your own words, about your needs and your concern for others. Prayer is also a way to say "thanks" to God for all of your blessings. When you pray, you should talk to God as you might talk to a friend. Tell God whatever is bothering you. Ask God to help you and to help others. Thank God for your many blessings. Prayer is a special way for you to talk to God.

Putting God Talk Into Action

Make a prayer chest. Give each child a cardboard chest or box. Have him or her decorate the box with jewels. Give each child several slips of paper and have him or her write a prayer request to God or the name of someone to pray for on each slip of paper. Instruct the child to put the slips of paper inside the prayer chest.

Encourage the children to take out slips of paper each day and pray for the persons whose names are written on the slips of paper or for the written prayer requests.

Prayer

Thank you, God, for the gift of prayer. Teach us how to pray. Help us to pray each day. Amen.

God Talk Reminder

Write the prayer requests for preschool children as they tell them to you. Jewels can be a choking hazard, so have them use peel-off stickers.

God's Promise to Abraham

Bible Verse
Then the LORD took Abram outside and said, "Look at the sky and see if you can count the stars. That's how many descendants you will have."
(Genesis 15:5, CEV)

Talk Point
God blesses you in many ways and always keeps God's promises to you.

Items Needed
black construction paper, star stickers, chalk and sidewalk chalk, Genesis 15:5 Scripture verse (page 81), glue

God Talk

Have you ever tried to count the stars in the night sky? It is impossible, isn't it! Abraham (Abram) was ninety-nine years old when God told him that his descendants (relatives) would be as many as the stars in the night sky. That is a lot of relatives. At the time, Abraham had no children. Yet, God kept the promise to Abraham when he and his wife Sarah were blessed with a son, Isaac. Isaac had his own children, and the family tree began to grow and grow.

God always keeps the promises God makes to you. God promises to always love you and care for you. God promises to direct your life and help you in difficult times. God promises to show you how to live each day in ways that are pleasing to God. God promises to guide you when you make choices in life.

God also blesses you in many ways, just as God blessed Abraham with many descendants. God blesses you with family, friends, and your church. God blesses you with many talents. God blesses you with a home, caring teachers, warm clothes, and good food to eat. God's blessings are so great that they are like the stars in the sky. You cannot count them!

Putting God Talk Into Action

Photocopy and cut out the Scripture verse (below). Give each child a piece of black construction paper and the Scripture verse. Instruct the children to glue the verses on their papers.

Give each child several star stickers. Have the children place their stars on the construction paper, leaving some room between stars. Give each child a piece of chalk and have him or her connect the stars.

Let the children go outside and draw stars on the sidewalk with the sidewalk chalk. Have them also draw pictures of ways God has blessed them. Offer suggestions to the children such as drawing pictures of family members, pets, home, school, friends, teachers, and church.

Prayer

Thank you, God, for blessing Abraham and his family. Thank you for keeping your promise to Abraham. Thank you God for our many blessings. Thank you, God, for always keeping your promises. Amen.

Then the LORD took Abram outside and said, "Look at the sky and see if you can count the stars. That's how many descendants you will have." (Genesis 15:5, CEV)

Then the LORD took Abram outside and said, "Look at the sky and see if you can count the stars. That's how many descendants you will have." (Genesis 15:5, CEV)

Then the LORD took Abram outside and said, "Look at the sky and see if you can count the stars. That's how many descendants you will have." (Genesis 15:5, CEV)

God Helps Isaac Find a Wife

Bible Verse

Abraham's servant did not say a word, but he watched everything Rebekah did, because he wanted to know for certain if this was the woman the LORD had chosen.

(Genesis 24:21, CEV)

Talk Point

God helped Isaac find a wife. God helps you make important decisions.

Items Needed

craft sticks, glue, tin can, slips of paper, pencils

God Talk

Tell the story of Isaac and Rebekah to the children. Explain that Isaac was the son of Abraham, the man that God promised to bless with many descendants (relatives).

It is time for Isaac to find a wife. Abraham, Isaac's father, wants to make sure that just the right woman is selected for Isaac. Abraham sends his trusted servant to travel to the land where Abraham was born. Abraham wishes for Isaac to marry a woman from among his relatives. The servant knows that his selection is very important. He prays to God to help him find Isaac the best wife from among Abraham's kinfolk.

The servant quickly learns that a woman named Rebekah is a kind and caring person. When the servant arrives at a well, Rebekah is there and she is getting water for her family. The servant and his camels are very thirsty and tired from their travels. The servant asks Rebekah for a drink of water. Rebekah gladly gives him water to quench his thirst. She then pours out water for the thirsty camels and goes back and forth to the well to get water until the camels drink all of the water they need and they are no longer thirsty. Rebekah goes out of her way to show kindness to the servant and to his animals. The thoughtful deeds convince the servant that Rebekah is a person who can be trusted.

Rebekah agrees to travel with the servant back to where Isaac lives and to become Isaac's wife. Her family approves of her marriage. Upon his return, the servant tells Isaac about his encounter with Rebekah at the well. Isaac wishes to marry Rebekah, and he loves her as his wife.

In our Bible story, the servant has an important decision to make. Before he decides to choose Rebekah for Isaac's wife, he prays to God to help him select the right person. What big decisions will you have to make in your life? *(college, future job, who they will marry, where they will live when they are adults)* Remember to pray to God before making any important decision. Like Abraham's servant, ask God to guide you.

Putting God Talk Into Action

Give each child a tin can and craft sticks. Let him or her glue the craft sticks around the tin can to make a well. Remind the children that Isaac's servant met Rebekah at a well. Give the children slips of paper and have him or her write down some important decisions in their own lives. These might be future decisions or something that each child must decide in the present moment. Have the children place their slips of paper inside the wells. Remind the children to pray to God to help them with their decisions.

Prayer

God, you helped Isaac's servant when he had an important decision to make. Please help us with any important decisions in our lives. We will pray before we make any important decisions. Amen.

God Talk Reminder

Help preschoolers glue their craft sticks to their cans. Let preschoolers tell you some of their present day chores rather than decisions. You might center in on some of the chores of preschoolers such as making their beds, feeding their dog, or helping set the table for dinner.

GODtalk

Abraham the Peacemaker

Bible Verse

Abram said to Lot, "We are close relatives. We shouldn't argue, and our men shouldn't be fighting one another. There is plenty of land for you to choose from. Let's separate. If you go north, I'll go south; if you go south, I'll go north."

(Genesis 13:8-9, CEV)

Talk Point

God wants you to be a peacemaker.

Items Needed

medium size jar, wax paper, rubber bands, crayons or markers, glue or tape, label (page 85), scissors

God Talk

Abraham had a nephew named Lot. Lot traveled with Abraham. Both men had many cattle, sheep, and goats. Both were wealthy men. When Abraham and Lot arrived at a certain place in their travels together, they had to make an important decision. They needed to separate because there was not enough pastureland left for both men.

Each man owned many animals and had many servants. Lot and Abraham's fellow travelers began to fight and quarrel with one another. Abraham knew that God did not want the men to argue with one another. Abraham decided to allow Lot to have the first choice in the area in which the two men would travel. Wherever Lot chose, Abraham would choose the other area in which to travel and settle down with his family.

God was pleased with Abraham because he was unselfish and allowed Lot to chose which direction he wanted to travel and live. Abraham was a peacemaker and refused to argue with Lot.

God wants you to get along with other people. We are often tempted to argue with others. God does not want people to fight with each other. Your unselfish actions toward others makes God very happy.

Putting God Talk Into Action

Photocopy and cut out the labels printed below. Give each child a jar and a label. Encourage the children to decorate the labels with crayons or markers. Show the children how to glue or tape the labels around the jars.

Cut a piece of wax paper to cover the opening of each jar. Help each child secure the wax paper to the top of the jar using a rubber band. Cut an opening in the top of the wax paper for each child.

Whenever the child avoids a fight or quarrel with others or whenever he or she practices peace, encourage the child to place a penny in the jar. When the jar is full, encourage the child to give the pennies to an organization that promotes peace.

Prayer

Dear God, help us to show peace toward others. Help us not to argue and fight with others. Thank you, God, for groups that work toward peace in our world today. Amen.

Pennies for Peace

Pennies for Peace

The Ten Commandments

Bible Verse

Moses called together the people of Israel and said: Today I am telling you the laws and teachings that you must follow, so listen carefully.
(Deuteronomy 5:1, CEV)

Talk Point

God gave us the Ten Commandments as rules for us to follow.

Items Needed

posterboard, tablet pattern (page 88), Ten Commandments (page 88), large athletic shoeboxes, peel-off jewels, glue, scissors

God Talk

Cut out ten tablets using the tablet pattern (page 88). Write one of the Ten Commandments on each tablet. Write what the commandment means on the back.

Commandment	Meaning
1. Do not worship any god except me.	We are only to worship God.
2. Do not worship idols.	Do not worship other things besides God.
3. Do not swear.	Do not misuse God's name.
4. Honor the Sabbath.	Take time on Sunday to rest and worship.
5. Honor your father and mother.	Respect your parents.
6. Do not murder.	Do not kill.
7. Be faithful in marriage.	Be faithful to the person you marry.
8. Do not steal.	Do not take what is not yours.
9. Do not tell lies about others.	Always be honest.
10. Do not envy what others own.	Do not want anything that belongs to others.

You have rules to follow in school and at home. What are some rules you have to follow at school? *(Let the children respond.)* What are some rules you have to follow at home? *(Let the children respond.)* These rules are set by your teachers and parents in order to keep you safe.

Adults have rules to follow as well. When your parents are driving their cars they have to follow certain traffic rules. They have to stop at a stop sign. They have to stop when the traffic light turns red. These traffic rules are a part of the law because without them your parents and other drivers would not be safe while driving their cars.

In the Bible, God gave us some rules to help us live each day. These rules are called the Ten Commandments. God gave the rules to Moses, the leader of the Jewish people. Moses took the Ten Commandments and shared them with the people.

Show the children your Ten Commandments tablets. Share with the children the Ten Commandments and the meaning of each commandment.

Putting God Talk Into Action
Photocopy and cut out the tablet pattern and the Ten Commandments (page 88) for each child. Give each child the tablet pattern and posterboard. Have the child use the pattern to cut out two tablets from the posterboard.

Give each child the Ten Commandments. Have the children glue the Ten Commandments to their two tablets. Let the children talk about ways they obey and disobey the commandments.

Give each child a shoebox. Explain that when the Jewish people and Moses traveled in the wilderness, they carried the Ten Commandments in a special box called the Ark of the Covenant. Let the children decorate their shoeboxes and use them to house their Ten Commandments tablets.

Prayer
Thank you, God, for the Ten Commandments. Help me to follow them so that I can live a happy life and treat others with love and respect. Amen.

God Talk Reminder
Cut out the tablets for preschool children and let them glue the Ten Commandments to them. Jewels can pose a choking hazard for young children. Use peel-off stickers instead.

1. Do not worship any god except me.
2. Do not worship idols.
3. Do not swear.
4. Honor the Sabbath.
5. Honor your father and mother.

6. Do not murder.
7. Be faithful in marriage.
8. Do not steal.
9. Do not tell lies about others.
10. Do not envy what others own.

God Calls Samuel

Bible Verse

The LORD then stood beside Samuel and called out as he had done before, "Samuel! Samuel!" "I'm listening," Samuel answered. "What do you want me to do?"

(1 Samuel 3:10, CEV)

Talk Point

God called Samuel for a special purpose, and God calls you for a special purpose.

Items Needed

paper towel tubes, wrapping paper, yellow tissue paper, glitter or glitter glue, tape, white glue, scissors

God Talk

Samuel was a young boy who was a helper in God's house. He helped the priest Eli light the candles and keep them burning. He was a good helper.

One night Samuel was sleeping when a voice woke him up. He thought it was the priest Eli, so he went to Eli's room and said, "Here I am. What do you want?" Eli answered, "I did not call you. Go back to bed." Samuel repeated his actions three times, and then Eli realized that God was calling Samuel. He told Samuel that the next time he heard the voice speaking to him to answer, "I'm listening, Lord. What do you want me to do?" The next time Samuel heard the voice speaking to him, he did exactly what Eli told him to do.

God had a plan for Samuel. God wanted Samuel to tell the people how God wanted them to live. When Samuel grew older he did exactly what God instructed him to do.

Eli helped Samuel know what God wanted him to do. Today parents, friends, pastors, and teachers help us understand what God wants us to do. Each of us have gifts to share with others. When we listen to people repeatedly tell us that we speak well, draw well, play a musical instrument well, or do anything else well, they help us recognize that we have talents that God can use.

Compliment each child in some way. When you offer them a compliment, ask them to say: "I'm listening, Lord. What do you want me to do?" (Example: "Sally you are kind. Mike, you play the piano well. Andrea, you draw very well. John, you read very well.")

Putting God Talk Into Action

Remind the children that Samuel served in God's house and helped to keep the candles burning. Encourage the children to share some ways they help others in their church and home.

Cut wrapping paper to fit the paper towel tubes. Give each child a tube and a piece of wrapping paper. Let the children cover their tubes with the wrapping paper. Help the children tape the wrapping paper onto the tubes. Let the children decorate their tubes with glitter.

Cut 6-inch squares from yellow tissue paper. Show children how to bunch up the tissue paper and place it in the tops of the cardboard tubes. Let the children take their candle to remind them of the way Samuel helped Eli and the ways they can help God today.

Prayer

God, Samuel listened to Eli. Help us to listen to others who help teach us what you want us to do. Amen.

David Fights a Giant

Bible Verse

You've come out to fight me with a sword and a spear and a dagger. But I've come out to fight you in the name of the LORD All-Powerful.

(1 Samuel 17:45, CEV)

Talk Point

God helped David defeat the giant Goliath. God helps you fight the huge problems in your life that seem like giants.

Items Needed

margarine containers, smooth water stones, blue felt scraps, glue, crayons, man's heavy coat, slips of paper, pens, scissors, picture of David (page 93)

God Talk

David was a shepherd boy who carefully watched over his sheep. He used his shepherd's stick (rod) to keep bears and wolves away from the sheep. He also had a sling shot. When he put stones inside the slingshot he would hurl them very fast at an attacking animal and keep his sheep safe from harm.

David's brothers were fighting in a war against the Philistines. A giant named Goliath, who was about nine feet tall, kept making fun of the nation of Israel. He kept saying mean words. At that time, the people believed that making fun of their nation was the same as making fun of God. Goliath's angry words upset the people very much, but everyone was too afraid of Goliath to do anything about his unkind words and actions.

One day David was visiting his brothers at the place where they were fighting. When he heard about Goliath, he volunteered to fight him! At first King Saul would not let him, but since there was no one else who wanted to fight Goliath, Saul decided to give David a try.

Saul fitted David with his armor and sword. However it was too big for David. David could hardly move. *Let the children take turns trying on the man's coat which will be much too large for them and weight them down like the king's armor weighted down David. When a child puts on the coat, have him or her say, like David did in I Samuel 17:39, CEV, "I can't move with all this stuff on."* David took off the king's armor and gave him back his sword. He took his own slingshot and found five stones. He prayed to God for help. David defeated the giant Goliath.

Do you ever have situations happen in your life that are so large that they seem like giants? God helps you defeat your problems and gives you strength to get through hard times. Like David, you must pray and ask God for help. Often God sends other people to help you and pray alongside you. Even though some times and situations may be tough for you, you should always turn to God and not give up.

Putting God Talk Into Action
Give each child a margarine container. Have him or her take off the top and lay it aside. Have the children glue scraps of blue felt inside the margarine container. Tell the children that the felt can remind them of the brook water where David found his five stones.

Give the children five smooth stones and five slips of paper. Encourage each child to write a problem they want to pray about on each slip. Have the children glue a slip to each stone and then place the stone in the margarine container.

Photocopy and cut out the picture of David (page 93) for each child. Let the children glue the picture onto their lids. Instruct the children to put the tops on the margarine containers.

Suggest to the children that they put the containers next to their beds. Each night before they go to sleep they can look at the stones and pray about each problem.

Prayer
God, help us when we face situations in life that seem giant-like. Thank you for helping David. Thank you for helping us. Amen.

God Talk Reminder
Smooth stones can be a choking hazard for young children who may put them into their mouths. Let younger children make their stones from brown play dough that they roll up into a ball. Let them place their play dough stones in their containers. Talk about things they can pray about, but do not write on the play dough stones.

A Kind Man Helps Ruth

Bible Verse

Naomi said, "Where did you work today? Whose field was it? God bless the man who treated you so well!" Then Ruth told her that she had worked in the field of a man named Boaz.

(Ruth 2:19, CEV)

Talk Point

God needs you to care for the poor.

Items Needed

containers with plastic lids (labels removed); duct tape, electrical tape or masking tape in a variety of colors; stalks of wheat, scissors, leftover bread

God Talk

Recruit a volunteer to dress in biblical costume to play the role of Ruth. Bring in some stalks of wheat to show the children. Give each child some stalks to hold. Explain the custom of gleaning—leaving some grain in the field for the poor to pick up to use for food.

Ruth: Good morning boys and girls. My name is Ruth. I traveled to Bethlehem to live with my mother-in-law, Naomi, after my husband's death. I was loyal to her, and I insisted that she let me remain with her even though I was not from her country. When we arrived in Bethlehem, we were very poor and needed food. I went into a field to gather some grain that was left over by the workers who had been busy harvesting. A man named Boaz saw me and he let me gather as much grain as I needed. He was kind to me. Later on he became my husband. Without his help my family would have been very hungry.

Have the children name ways they can help the poor in their community. Whenever a child names something, have him or her give a stalk of wheat to Ruth. Have Ruth say words of thanks as she collects the wheat stalk from each child. Some suggestions: "Thank you for helping me." "You are very kind." "Now I can bake bread and not be hungry." "Without your help, I would be very hungry." "Thank you for helping the poor."

Putting God Talk Into Action

Cut a slit in the plastic lid of each container. Give each child a container and lid. Let the children cover their containers with pieces of colored tape. Encourage the children to cover their entire containers.

Instruct the children to collect money and place in their containers. They might collect from friends or family or do chores to make money. Select a date for the children to turn in their money. Let the children help you decide where the money will go.

Give the children a piece of leftover bread. Let them go outside and scatter the bread in places where the birds can find it. Encourage the children to use leftover bread at home to feed the birds. Remind them that Boaz and the harvest workers left grain in the field for the poor. Not only can we help hungry people, we can also help the birds that God created.

Prayer

God, help us to care for those that are hungry. Amen.

Esther Saves Her People

Bible Verse

"If you don't speak up now, we will somehow get help, but you and your family will be killed. It could be that you were made queen for a time like this!"

(Esther 4:14, CEV)

Talk Point

God used Esther to help save her people. God can use you to speak out for what is right and wrong.

Items Needed

crown front (page 97), markers, peel-off jewels or stickers, glue, construction paper

God Talk

Photocopy and cut out the crown front (page 97) for each child. Give the children crowns to hold as you share with them the story of Esther.

King Xerxes decided that he needed a new queen. Many beautiful women were selected to come to the palace. Esther, a Jewish girl, was one of the women chosen to come to the palace. After several months, Esther became the new queen. Esther had a relative named Mordecai. Soon after she became queen, Mordecai told her that an evil man named Haman planned to kill all of the Jewish people. Mordecai asked Esther to go to the king and tell him about Haman's plans. At first Esther was afraid. She knew that she had to have permission from the king to enter his chambers. He had to stretch out his scepter in order for anyone to come into his room. If he did not extend his scepter, the person could be killed. But Esther went to the king even though she was afraid. The king allowed Esther to enter, and she invited the king to a party. At the party, she told the king about Haman's plans to destroy the Jewish people. The king was not happy when he heard about what Haman intended to do to the Jewish people. Esther's courage saved her people!

God wants us to speak out, like Esther, for what is right. It takes a great deal of courage to speak the truth to others. Yet, God helps us to have the courage to do what is right and to say what is right. Today is our time to tell the truth and to let others know that we want to follow the teachings of God in all of the situations we face in life. God selected Esther to be a leader in the time in which she lived. God selects us today to be a leader in the times in which we live.

Putting God Talk Into Action

Cut two strips of construction paper about 2 inches by 11 inches for each child. Tape or glue one of the strips to each side of the child's crown front to complete the crown. Measure the crown around the child's head and tape the ends of the side strips together.

Let the children decorate their crowns with markers, stickers, and peel-off jewels.

Prayer

Thank you, God, for helping us speak out for what is right and wrong. Give us courage to always speak the truth. Amen.

God Talk Reminder

Let the preschool children decorate their crowns with stickers and markers. Jewels can be a choking hazard for younger children.

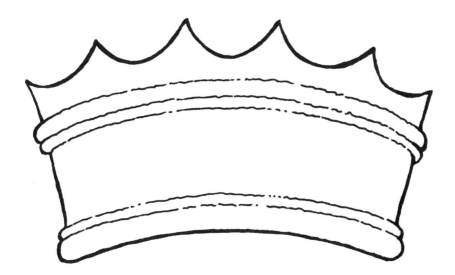

God Takes Care of All Creation

Bible Verse

You provide steams of water in the hills and valleys, so that the donkeys and other wild animals can satisfy their thirst. Birds build their nests nearby and sing in the trees.

(Psalm 104:10-12, CEV)

Talk Point

God takes care of all creation. God wants you to help take care of the animals God created.

Items Needed

cardboard milk or juice cartons, twigs, string, paint, paintbrushes, paint smocks, pencils, scissors, stapler, paper punch, pictures of different animals

God Talk

Show the children pictures of animals and let them identify the animals.

God created all of the animals. Animals provide us food, help us with our work, and assist us in many important ways. Trained dogs help police officers and assist in rescue efforts. Animals help people in nursing homes, guide the blind, and assist other persons who are in need. Animals are also pets and family members. How many of you have a pet in your family? *(Let the children respond.)* God depends on you to take care of your pet and provide your pet with food and water. In nature, God created streams where the wild animals can go and find water when they are thirsty. God created trees so the birds can live in the trees and build their nests. The writer of the Psalms tells us that God created a beautiful world, and all of the animals are provided with water, trees, mountains, and rocks.

All animals need water and food. Animals also search for a good place to make their homes. Some animals need the trees for a home. What animals are these? *(birds)* Some animals need to make their home on a mountain.

What animals are these? *(goats)* Small animals can hide under rocks and use them for a home. What animals are these? *(bugs)* Other animals make their home in the grass. What animals are these? *(cattle)* Animals also live in barns. What animals are these? *(horses)*

God created people to help take care of the animals. Some people take care of animals in the zoo. Farmers take care of animals on their farms. You take care of your pets when you feed them, walk them, and pet them.

When the winter comes, you can help God take care of the birds. During the spring and summer, birds can easily find worms to eat, but in the winter it is much harder for the birds to find food. Some people help God take care of the birds by putting bird feeders or bird houses in their yards. Whatever you decide to do to help take care of the animals, God is very pleased with your efforts.

Putting God Talk Into Action

Invite a police officer along with his canine partner, a rescue dog and owner, or a therapy dog and owner. Let this person tell the children about the care of the animal and the work of the animal. Caution children to never pet an animal without the owner's permission. If this type of animal is not available, bring in a friendly and gentle animal for the children to pet.

Make a birdhouse: Let the children go outside and find their own twigs, one for each child. Give each child a cardboard milk or juice carton. Help the children staple the top of the cardboard container until it is tightly shut. Assist the children with cutting a hole in the side of their cartons to make a doorway for the birds. Help the children use pencils to poke holes in either side of their cartons. Have the children push their twigs through both holes so the birds will have a perch. Help the children poke holes in the bottom of their cartons for drainage. Let the children paint their birdhouses. While they are drying, have the invited guest share with the children. When the paint is dry, help the children punch a hole in the top of their cartons. Have them thread a piece of string through the holes of the cartons. Encourage the children to hang their birdhouses outside filled with birdseeds or bread crumbs.

Prayer

Thank you, God, for creating the animals and providing them with water and places to make their homes. Help us to take good care of the animals you created. Amen.

Obey Your Parents

Bible Verse
My child, obey the teachings of your parents, and wear their teachings as you would a lovely hat or a pretty necklace.
(Proverbs 1:8-9, CEV)

Talk Point
The Bible teaches you to obey your parents.

Items Needed
cardboard, aluminum foil, tape, paper punch, ribbon, peel-off decorations, inexpensive sun visors, markers

God Talk

What are some things your parents do to show you love? *(feed me, go to my activities at school, help me with homework, provide our family with a nice home, hug me)* Parents do many things to help their children. Parents teach you right from wrong. Parents work very hard at their jobs in order to have money to buy food, clothes, and toys for you. Parents spend time helping you with homework, school projects, or other activities. Parents teach you about God and Jesus. Parents love you, share with you, and pray for you. Parents want what is best for you. They want you to grow up to be wonderful and happy adults.

The Bible instructs children to obey their parents. You obey your parents when you do what they ask you to do without complaining. You obey your parents when you act in a kind way and use your manners, rather than act unkind and rude to others. You obey your parents when you do the good and right things they have taught you and turn away from what you know to be wrong. Obeying your parents pleases God.

Putting God Talk Into Action
Explain to the children that the Bible teaches us to follow our parents' teachings. When we do, others can see that we are being obedient to our parents just like they would notice if we were wearing a pretty necklace or lovely hat. Let the children make both a necklace and a hat. Encourage the child to give the necklace to his or her mother and the visor to his or

her father. Be sensitive of children who have lost a parent. Suggest they give their gifts to someone else who is special and important to them.

Necklace: Cut a piece of cardboard into a small rectangular shape for each child. Show the child how to cover the cardboard piece with aluminum foil. Secure the back edges of the foil with tape. Help each child punch a hole in one pointed end of the rectangular shape and tie a ribbon long enough to fit around the child's neck. Let the children decorate their necklaces with peel-off stickers.

Hat: Give each child a visor. Let the children decorate with markers.

Prayer
Thank you, God, for our parents. Help us to obey them. Amen.

Good Works

Bible Verse
Faith that doesn't lead us to do good deeds is all alone and dead!
(James 2:17, CEV)

Talk Point
Your faith leads you to do good deeds for others.

Items Needed
resealable plastic bags, ribbon, packaged muffin mixes (you will need two muffins for each child), ingredients needed to make muffins, muffin pans, muffin papers, construction paper, markers or crayons

God Talk

What we believe about God, Jesus, and the Bible is important. We believe in a great God who loves us. We believe in Jesus, God's Son, who was born as a baby, lived and taught on earth, died on a cross, and now lives! We believe in the Holy Spirit who helps us follow God's teachings. We call these beliefs our faith.

The writer of the book of James teaches us that your faith leads you to do good deeds. Because we love God and Jesus, we want to reach out and help those in need. A follower of Jesus wants to share the love of God with others. A follower of Jesus shows kindness, especially to people who are sick, poor, hungry, or find themselves in difficult situations in life. James knew that it was impossible to be a follower of Jesus unless we treated others in the ways Jesus taught us. Your faith leads you to do good deeds for others.

What good deeds can you do to help another person? Think about your neighborhood. Do you have some elderly neighbors you could help? Perhaps you could help your neighbors rake their leaves, help them carry in groceries, or volunteer to walk their pets.

Think about your church. Is there someone who needs cheering up? Could you send those people get-well cards and take them some baked goods? Is there a new child that you could sit with during worship?

Think about your school. Is there some way you could help your teacher? Is there a new student that would like a friend?

When you look around you can find many people who just need a kind word or a smile from a child. That child could be you! When you share good deeds with others you also share your faith in Jesus.

Putting God Talk Into Action

Let the children help you prepare muffins. Give the children different tasks: measuring, putting the muffin papers into the muffin pans, stirring, and putting the muffin mixture into the muffin pans.

While the muffins are cooking, give each child two pieces of construction paper. Show the children how to fold their paper in half to make cards for people in need. Let the children decorate their cards with markers. Encourage the children to write notes.

Talk to the children about ways they have helped others in the past. Praise the children for their efforts.

Invite a visitor to come and share with the children about a mission project.

After the muffins have cooled, give each child two resealable plastic bags, two muffins, and two pieces of ribbon. Have each child place a muffin in each bag and tie it with a ribbon. Encourage the children to give their muffins and cards to people in need such as a friend who has lost a loved one, a friend in the hospital, or a family with a new baby.

Prayer

God, we want to do good deeds because of our faith in Jesus. Amen.

Everything Belongs to God

Bible Verse

The earth and everything on it belong to the LORD. The world and its people belong to him.

(Psalm 24:1, CEV)

Talk Point

God created the world and its people. The world belongs to God. All the people in the world belong to God. You belong to God.

Items Needed

paper lunch bags, plastic garbage bag, shoeboxes, plastic wrap, tape, nature items, glue, pictures of nature and pictures of people from around the world

God Talk

Show the children pictures of nature. Show the children pictures of people from different parts of the world.

You live in a beautiful world created by a wonderful, loving God. God made everything you see in nature including trees, plants, water, sky, and animals. All of nature belongs to God.

God made all of the people of the world. These people speak many different languages, wear various kinds of clothes, and live in many countries throughout the world, but they are all children of God. God loves all of the people of the world. All of the people of the world belong to God. You belong to God, also.

Whenever you go outside and view God's beautiful world, you should thank God. You should also try to keep God's world clean. If you see trash, pick it up, throw it away, or recycle. Never throw trash on the ground. Take care of the animals God created. The world belongs to God, and God expects you to help take care of the world.

There are many different kinds of people in the world. Whenever you meet someone who lives in a different country from you or speaks a different language, you should treat these friends with respect. Never make fun of other people who are not like you. Learn to appreciate the customs, dress, and food of other people. Remember that these people belong to God as much as you belong to God.

Ask the children to clap several times after each phrase to give God claps of praise and thanks:

The trees belong to God.
The grass belongs to God.
Animals belong to God.
The clouds belong to God.
All the people of the world belong to God.
The sky belongs to God.
The birds belong to God.
You belong to God.

Let the children add other phrases that describe things that belong to God. Have them to continue clapping after each phrase.

Putting God Talk Into Action

Give each child a paper lunch bag and let him or her go on a nature scavenger hunt. Suggest items to place in the lunch bag such as grass, a pinecone, a cloverleaf, a wildflower, a twig, a small rock, an acorn, a nut, or a leaf. Remind the children to never disturb the home of any animal and to avoid picking flowers in a garden. Take a plastic sack with you and encourage the children to pick up any trash they see and put it in the plastic sack.

After items are collected, give each child a shoebox. Let the children glue their nature items to the inside bottom of the shoeboxes and on the small sides. Have the children turn their shoeboxes with the open side toward them. Give each child a piece of plastic wrap to cover the open space and help the child tape it to the sides of the box. The children can look at their nature diorama and be reminded that the world belongs to God.

Prayer

God, we praise you for making a beautiful world. We are glad the world belongs to you. We are happy we belong to you. Amen.

Jesus Calms the Storm

Bible Verse

He got up and gave orders to the wind, and he said to the lake, "Silence! Be still!" The wind settled down and there was a great calm.

(Mark 4:39, CEB)

Talk Point

Jesus calms you when you are afraid. Jesus brings peace into your life.

Item Needed

margarine containers (without lids), drinking straws, play dough, crayons or markers, scissors, paper punch, sail (page 107)

God Talk

Teach the children sign language for peace. (Hands are clasped together, and then reverse hands until the other hand is on top. Then open both hands and move them downward and outward away from the body with fingers apart.) Practice this with the children several times. Tell the children to make a sound like the wind blowing whenever you say the word storm; *to sign the word for peace whenever you say the word* Jesus; *and to pretend they are rowing a boat when you use the word* boat.

Today I want to share with you a Bible story about **Jesus** *(sign the word for peace)* and his disciples. **Jesus** *(sign the word for peace)* and his disciples were in a **boat** *(rowing motion)* on the Sea of Galilee. Suddenly a terrible **storm** *(make sound like wind blowing)* started rocking their **boat** *(rowing motion)*. The **storm** *(make sound like wind blowing)* was so fierce that waves started splashing into the **boat** *(rowing motion)*. The **boat** *(rowing motion)* was about to sink. **Jesus** *(sign the word for peace)* was in the back of the **boat** *(rowing motion)* asleep during the **storm** *(make sound like wind blowing)*. The disciples of **Jesus** *(sign the word for peace)* were very afraid. They woke **Jesus** *(sign the word for peace)* and told him they were afraid. He got up and commanded the wind and the waves to be quiet. Everything was quiet and the **storm** *(make sound like wind blowing)* immediately stopped. The disciples calmed down and were amazed at the power of **Jesus** *(sign the word for peace)* because even the wind and the waves obeyed him.

Like the disciples, there are times when you are afraid. Sometimes you may be frightened during a thunderstorm. Maybe you find yourself scared when you have to face new things in your lives, like the first day of school, moving to a new home, or making new friends. When you are afraid, you can pray to Jesus. Jesus will help you to calm down. Jesus will help you feel peace.

Putting God Talk Into Action

Photocopy and cut out a sail (below) for each child. Let the children decorate the sails with crayons or markers. Help each child punch three holes along one side of the sail. Show the child how to weave a straw through the holes.

Give each child a margarine container (without a lid) and small amount of play dough. Have the children press the play dough into the bottom of the container and then attach the straw into the play dough.

Place a tub partially filled with water on the floor. Let the children try floating their margarine container boats in the water. Remind the children that several of Jesus' disciples were fishermen.

Prayer

Thank you, Jesus, for helping us calm down when we are frightened. We are glad that we can pray to you when we are afraid. You bring peace to our lives. Amen.

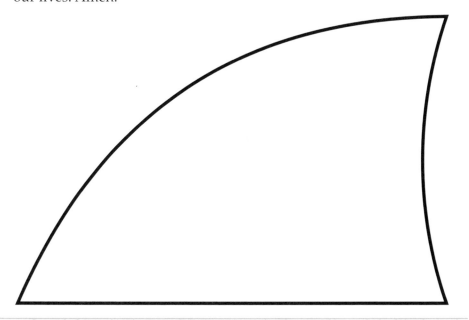

Deep Roots

Bible Verse

Plant your roots in Christ and let him be the foundation for your life. Be strong in your faith, just as you were taught. And be grateful.

(Colossians 2:7, CEV)

Talk Point

A plant grows when its roots are planted in good, fertile soil and when it receives water and sunlight. Jesus helps you grow strong in your faith, but you must love Jesus, pray to God, read your Bible, help others, and be thankful.

Items Needed

a healthy plant, clean empty soup or vegetable cans, small plants, potting soil, peel-off leaf stickers, newspaper

God Talk

Bring in a large healthy plant to show the children.

All plants have roots. Roots are found at the bottom of a plant and help the plant grow. My plant has good roots. How do I know that? Look how healthy the leaves are. I have taken good care of this plant. I watered it, gave it sunlight, and replanted it when needed. Sometimes I added some plant food to help my plant grow stronger. Healthy plants need replanting from time to time. When I replanted this plant, I took it out of a smaller container and planted it in a larger container. That way, the roots could continue to spread out and have room to help the plant grow even taller.

The Bible advises you to plant your roots in Jesus. The Scripture teaches you of the need to grow in your faith. The way to do that is to let Jesus have first place in your life. A plant grows when it is watered and given sunlight. You grow when you pray, read your Bible, and love Jesus. You grow when you learn Bible stories, Bible songs, and when you praise and worship God. You grow when you do kind things for other people. You should be very thankful for the many good ways to grow in your faith.

Putting God Talk Into Action

Give each child a can from which the label has been removed. Have the child decorate the can with peel-off leaf stickers.

Spread newspaper on the table and place some potting soil into each child's can. Give him or her a small plant to place in the can. Reinforce with more potting soil. Remind the children that if they care for their plants, they will eventually have to replant them into larger containers so they can continue to grow.

Remind the children that they will continue to grow when they read their Bible, pray, worship, help others, and love Jesus. Encourage the children to say a prayer of thanks for the ways they are growing in their faith whenever they water their plants.

Prayer

God, we want to grow stronger each day in our faith. We can do this when we love Jesus and do the things you want us to do. Help us take action to grow in the way you want us to grow. Amen.

Jesus Heals

Bible Verse

(Jesus said) "Get up! Pick up your mat and go home." The man got right up. He picked up his mat and went out while everyone watched in amazement. They praised God and said, "We have never seen anything like this!"

(Mark 2:11-12, CEV)

Talk Point

Jesus healed a man who could not walk. The man's friends took the time to bring him to Jesus, and Jesus was pleased with their faith. Today, Jesus is pleased when you go out of your way to help another friend know about Jesus and his love.

Items Needed

picture of Bible-times house, cardboard box, piece of fabric, cord or twine, small doll, a small box for each child, scissors or utility knife (adult use only), brown play dough or scraps of brown paper and glue

God Talk

Show the children a picture of a house during Jesus' time. Explain to the children that the roof was flat and there were steps up to the top floor of the house.

Prior to your time of sharing, take a piece of fabric and cut four slits in each corner of the fabric. Tie equal length pieces of cord or twine into the slits. Bring a cardboard box to use for the house. Decorate the outside of the box if you wish. Set the box in front of the children. Place a small doll on the mat beside the box house. The doll will represent the man who was carried to Jesus for healing.

Word spread quickly that Jesus was in the town of Capernaum. People were very excited when they learned that Jesus was in a house. Many people rushed to the house, and soon the house became so crowded that no one could get inside. Four friends tried to bring a man to see Jesus. The man was unable to walk, and the friends hoped that Jesus might heal the man. However, because of the huge crowds, the friends could not get to Jesus. Then, they had an idea. They carried the man up the steps of the house to the top floor. They cut a hole in the roof of the house and used the mat to lower the man down toward Jesus. Jesus praised the friends for their great faith. He told the man to get up, pick up his mat, and go home! The man did exactly as Jesus told him to do. The man was healed and able to walk again! All of the people were so surprised. They praised God and said, "We have never seen anything like this."

Open the flaps of your cardboard box (house) to represent the hole the friends cut into the roof of the house. Let the children take turns being friends and lowering the doll on the mat down into the box (house).

Jesus was pleased when the friends helped the man who could not walk. Jesus is pleased when you help others, especially when you tell them about Jesus and his love. It took time and effort to bring the man to Jesus. Sometimes helping others takes extra time and effort on your part.

Putting God Talk Into Action
Cut a small hole in the bottom of a small box for each child. Give each child a box. Show the child how to place the box so that the bottom becomes the roof of a house. Point out the hole in the roof. Remind the children that the four friends lowered the man through the roof in order to get the man to Jesus.

Let the children decorate the outside of their boxes to look like Bible-times homes. The children could glue scraps of brown construction paper on the box or they could cover the box with brown play dough. If you choose to use play dough, have the children firmly press the play dough onto the sides and roof of box house.

Prayer
God, we want to be good friends and tell others about Jesus. Amen.

Index